— THE —
HANDLOOM WEAVERS
AND THE
ULSTER LINEN INDUSTRY

W. H. CRAWFORD

Mairead

from

Will

£10

ULSTER
HISTORICAL FOUNDATION

W. H. (Bill) Crawford is a native of Coleraine, County Londonderry, and a product of its Model School and Academical Institution. After graduating from Dublin University he taught history for twelve years at Lurgan College and was introduced to archives through the Brownlow estate papers there. From 1966 he had responsibility for the education programme at the Public Record Office of Northern Ireland. In 1980 he became Keeper of Material Culture at the Ulster Folk and Transport Museum. Since 1993 he has been Development Officer for the Federation for Ulster Local Studies which he helped to found in 1975.

First published 1972 by
Gill and Macmillan Ltd

© W.H. Crawford 1994

This edition published 1994 by
The Ulster Historical Foundation
12 College Square East, Belfast BT1 6DD

Cover design by Wendy Dunbar

ISBN 0-901905-63-1

This book has received support from the Cultural Traditions Programme of the Community Relations Council, which aims to encourage acceptance and understanding of cultural diversity.

Printed by W & G Bairds Ltd

Contents

Acknowledgments

Grateful acknowledgment is made to the following for assistance in selection of illustrations and for permission to reproduce illustrations in this book.

National Library of Ireland; University of London; The Controller of Her Majesty's Stationery Office; Public Record Office of Northern Ireland; Linen Hall Library, Belfast; Ulster Museum; Ulster Architectural Heritage Society; Ulster Folk Museum; Century Newspapers Ltd; Armagh County Museum; National Trust Committee for Northern Ireland; An Taisce; William Clark & Sons, Ltd.

Preface

The first edition of this publication was written for a series 'Insights Into Irish History' published by Gill and Macmillan in 1972. Entitled *Domestic Industry in Ireland: The Experience of the Linen Industry*, it set out to explain the concept of domestic industry using the records that have survived from the Irish linen industry. As a result it concentrated on the experiences of the handloom weavers and their families as they tried to make a living and to cope with the major changes that occurred with the industrialisation of the industry throughout the nineteenth century. The new edition has provided an opportunity to provide a more relevant title: *The Handloom Weavers and the Ulster Linen Industry*. No significant changes have been made to the text of the original chapters and appendices but a bibliographical essay has been supplied and a new preface and introduction replace the original preface, introduction, and 'notes to teachers'.

Introduction

It is in the nature of man's memory to jettison those elements of history it no longer regards as relevant. Over time they disappear from our consciousness as if they never existed, no matter how significant they may have been for past generations. An example from our own past concerns the handloom weaving of linen and cotton for export to British and foreign markets. It is now a vague memory but once it was a fundamental feature of Ulster life. It accounted for the extraordinary density of population in Ulster which, on the eve of the Great Famine, was the highest in Ireland; in fact the population of Ulster according to the 1821 census was almost equal, at two millions, to that of the whole of Scotland. It was also a consequence of the domestic weaving industry that the average size of farms in Ulster remained the smallest in Western Europe as late as the early twentieth century, while the mileage of roads throughout the province exceeded that of any comparable region of Western Europe. These three features were interrelated. The practice of agreeing leases as contracts between landlord and tenant had been established under the terms of the Plantation but it was the success of the domestic linen industry, especially in the eighteenth century, that led to a long process of sub-dividing farms in the knowledge that the rent would be paid from the earnings of the loom. The availability of work for families encouraged their creation. The business that was generated by them revolutionised the finances for road construction raised by the county grand juries so that road-building became a valuable method of employing the poor. In time innovative practices became tradition and as part of our culture they continued to colour our opinions, attitudes and expectations.

The Irish linen industry gained an international reputation for the quality of its fabrics by winning many awards at the great international exhibitions held throughout the world in the late nineteenth century. It had a long pedigree for Irish linen yarn had been exported to Lancashire in the late medieval period though it was not until the late seventeenth century that it became a significant commercial commodity on the London market.[1] By 1730 it had established itself there against continental linens and continued to grow throughout the rest of the century.[2] Exports to England rose from four million yards in the 1720s to 16 million in the 1760s and 42 million by the early 1800s.[3] Its success was due to the low cost of living in both the spinning and weaving districts and this advantage became more pronounced when bleachers, by adapting methods from the fulling and finishing of woollens, established bleach mills driven by water power to reduce the cost of bleaching.[4] As a result the bleachers began to dominate the industry, encouraging the Board of Trustees of the Linen and Hempen Manufacturers to promote public markets in towns with paid officials, denominated 'sealmasters', to examine and approve the quality of unbleached linens brought for sale.[5] The bleachers sent their buyers, known as linen drapers, from market to market throughout the province to buy varieties of linen from which to process and fulfil orders from England. Competition to reduce bleaching costs compelled these firms to increase their annual output from about 1,000 webs in the 1750s to almost 10,000 webs after 1800, while the smaller firms were forced out of business. Irish bleaching was regarded highly by competitors: from more than 350 greens in 1787 the number fell to 295 in 1803, 130 by 1830 and just over 40 by the mid 1850s.[6]

If the bleachers were the entrepreneurs and managers of the domestic linen industry, the spinners and weavers were the country people who sought to make a better living by taking up the industry. The technology of spinning and weaving changed very little over more than a century – Ulster linen weavers did not adopt the flying shuttle until 1825. It must be concluded, therefore, that the increasing exports of linen in the same period reflect the vast numbers of women who took up spinning and of men who became weavers. When the bleachers needed more cloth they sent their drapers further afield to markets in the west and south of the province such as Strabane, Newtownstewart and Omagh in Co. Tyrone and Cootehill and Ballibay in Cos Cavan and Monaghan.[7] These markets became even more important when cotton weaving on the handloom displaced linen weaving all around Belfast Lough after the 1780s: a cotton weaver could earn twice as much as a linen weaver. Yet because the large bleach greens represented such major investments of capital, the linens were carried to them. During the 1780s, when they built the White Linen Hall, the Belfast merchants organised the export of linens so effectively that they managed to outdo their rivals in Newry and gradually displaced Dublin as the capital of the trade over the next half-century.[8]

Public markets for the sale of linen cloth and yarn were characteristic of the linen industry in Ulster. In Scotland, by contrast, much of the raw material was imported from the Baltic, processed and put out to weavers who worked to specifications. In Ireland it was not possible for merchants to control the supply of raw materials because too much linen yarn was spun by the women on the farms where it had been grown. They prepared it to meet official standards and then it was carried by 'grey yarn jobbers' to the cloth markets. There it was sold to the weavers who needed to buy it once they had received cash for their webs. The public markets survived in Ulster as long as hand-spun linen yard was available because they suited the needs of both the merchants and the weavers. The merchants were able to purchase the range of linens that they required by sending their buyers on regular tours around the markets. The weavers believed that competition between the buyers ensured the best price for their work.[9]

The introduction of mill spinning of linen yarns marked the first major stage in the industrialisation of the industry. The mill owners had learned from the experiences of the cotton industry which had been introduced into Belfast in the 1780s. Cotton was imported either as yarn or as cotton wool to be spun in new multi-storied mills driven by water or steam power. Mill-spun yarn was preferable to hand-spun because it was more even and hence easier to weave. The yard was then put out to handloom weavers who wove it and then brought the finished webs back to the office for payment. There they were fined for the flaws and for days overdue. They were in no position to object because they had become dependent on the mill owners for their livelihood. They were especially vulnerable when trade was bad and wages were cut.[10]

Yet it was the introduction of the wet spinning process for producing fine linen yarns in the late 1820s that saved the Ulster linen industry from extinction at the hands of rival firms in England and Scotland. Contemporary observers in the mid 1820s forecast the destruction of the industry but within ten years there were twenty-seven flax spinning mills operating. This success was due to the expansion of the manufacture of cambrics (mainly for handkerchiefs but also for underclothing) that had developed in the Lurgan area by 1775 and spread through a ten-mile radius in 1803.[11] The skill of these weavers, who are considered to have numbered some 13,000 by 1854, enabled Ulster to seize the initiative in the British Isles and even in the international markets. In 1857 it was reckoned, for instance, that 'in 1829 for every 1,000 dozen pieces of French cambric sold in the English market 100 pieces of Irish were sold; in 1846, for every 1,000 pieces of French there were 16,000 pieces of Irish sold.'[12] Even then a wide variety of linens was produced throughout the province:

> Coarse linens for blouses, etc., and for the common kinds of export goods are chiefly made in the county of Armagh; medium and fine kinds of export cloth about Ballymena and Coleraine; damasks and diapers at Lurgan, Lisburn and Belfast; lawns at Lurgan and Dromore; cambrics at Lurgan, Waringstown, and Dromore; heavy linens and sheetings for the home market at Banbridge; hollands in the counties of Antrim and Armagh; shirt fronts, woven in plaits at Dromore; and the coarsest fabrics, such as bed-ticks, coarse drills, etc., at Drogheda.[13]

This period saw the production of some of the finest linen cloths ever woven, triumphs of the weavers' skill. Before the introduction of powerlooms led to the standardisation of production, firms competed to produce inimitable specimens for international exhibitions. At the Great Exhibition of 1851, for example, John Henning of Waringstown gained a gold medal by exhibiting a plain cambric web that was reckoned to be the finest yet woven anywhere: fifty feet in length, it was folded and sent to the bleachers in a moderate-size envelope. It is significant, however, that at least another twenty-five Ulster firms showed linens at this exhibition and won many awards.[14]

Among these establishments were the great bleaching firms that continued to dominate the industry. A very knowledgeable Belgian visitor recognised in 1846 that 'the bleachers constitute a class of industrialists that I consider as important as the spinners'.

He concluded:

> The business of exporting in Ireland is for the most part in the hands of the bleachers. There are bleachers who bleach for the public and others who bleach only for themselves. They buy unfinished cloth from manufacturers, bleach it and finish it according to the tastes of different markets where it is sent on their own account. They have agents in the principal parts of the world, namely in the United States, in Mexico, in Chile, etc. This class of industrialists is very important and has a large capital. It does not exist in Belgium.[15]

By 1870 this class was establishing its headquarters around the White Linen Hall in Donegall Square and then in the great warehouses in Bedford Street and Linenhall Street. It master-minded the introduction of the powerlooms and constructed the factories to house them: their numbers increased from 58 to 1850 to 4,108 in 1862 and 12,419 in 1868. This rapid acceleration was due to the American Civil War when the cessation of cotton supplies to Britain forced customers to purchase linens as a substitute.[16]

The powerlooms soon undermined the world of the handloom weavers, both in linen cambrics and cottons, because they drove down the cost of weaving. A great exodus from the weaving districts ensued as weavers abandoned their looms and left with their families. A study of a handloom weaving district in north-east Down indicates that in the half century between 1861 and 1911 this densely populated community lost more than half of its population and 40% of its housing stock at double the rate suffered by Co. Down altogether.[17] First to go were the cambric weavers because powerlooms were soon adapted to weave fine yarns. The damask weavers, however, survived into the 1960s because powerlooms could not match the quality of the hand-woven damasks. In time demand for hand-woven damasks declined because the cost of labour was too high even when all the weavers were old-age pensioners.

Nevertheless, although the handloom weaving trade died, its vestiges remain. A comparison of successive editions of the Ordnance Survey maps, or of the decennial census returns, reminds us not only of the families that have gone but of the farms that have survived. Compared with other regions of Britain many homes are still occupied throughout the countryside. Although farms have been bought in and consolidated into larger units many smallholders were able to retain holdings by obtaining employment in neighbouring towns. Although the construction of rural houses has changed dramatically with the disappearance of thatch, the pattern of small fields persists throughout the province while the network of roads still penetrates everywhere.

Footnotes to Introduction

1. W.H. Crawford, 'The origins of the linen industry in north Armagh and the Lagan Valley', *Ulster Folklife*, 12 (1967), pp.42–4; J. Thirsk and J.P. Cooper, eds, *Seventeenth-century economic documents* (Oxford, 1972), pp.302, 303.

2. N.B. Harte, 'The rise of protection and the English linen trade, 1690–1790' in N.B. Harte and K.G. Ponting, eds, *Textile history and economic history* (Manchester, 1973), pp.94–5, 102.

3. C. Gill, *The rise of the Irish linen industry* (Oxford, 1925), pp.341–2.

4. W.H. Crawford, 'Drapers and bleachers in the early Ulster linen industry' in L.M. Cullen and P. Butel, eds, *Négoce et industrie en France et en Irlande aux xviiie et xixe siècles* (Paris, 1980), pp.113–9.

5. W.H. Crawford, 'The evolution of the linen trade of Ulster before industrialisation', *Irish Economic and Social History XV* (1988), pp.42–5.

6. A. L'Amie, 'Chemicals in the eighteenth-century Irish linen industry' (M.S.Sc. thesis, Queen's University, Belfast, 1984); Crawford, 'Evolution of the linen trade of Ulster', p.37; W.A. McCutcheon, *The Industrial Archaeology of Northern Ireland* (Belfast, 1980), p.292; PRONI D.562/6225.

7. W.H. Crawford, 'Evolution of the linen trade of Ulster,' pp.49–50 loc. cit.

8. W.H. Crawford, 'Change in Ulster in the late eighteenth century' in T. Bartlett and D.W. Hayton, eds, *Penal Era and Golden Age* (Belfast, 1979), pp.192–6.

9. Crawford, 'Evolution of the linen trade of Ulster', pp.39–40 loc. cit.

10. E.R.R. Green, 'The cotton hand-loom weavers in the north-east of Ireland', *Ulster Journal of Archaeology*, 3rd ser., 7 (1944), pp.30–41.

11. Arthur Young, *A tour of Ireland*, ed. A.W. Hutton (2 vols, London, 1892), I, p.128.

12. A. Ure, *Philosophy of manufacturers or an exposition of the scientific, moral, and commercial economy of the factory system of Great Britain*, 3rd edition continued in its details to the present time by P.L. Simmonds (London, 1861), p.600.

13. ibid., p.599.

14. H. McCall, *Ireland and her staple manufactures* (3rd edition, Belfast, 1870), pp.275–6; Official description and illustrated catalogue of the Great Exhibition 1851 (4 vols, London, 1851), pp.510–1, 516.

15. P. Solar, 'A Belgian view of the Ulster linen industry in the 1840s', *Ulster Folklife* 34 (1988), pp.23, 24.

16. H.D. Gribbon, *The history of water power in Ulster* (Newton Abbot, 1969), p.101.

17. W.H. Crawford, 'A handloom weaving community in County Down', *Ulster Folklife* 39 (1993).

The Rise of the Linen Industry in the Eighteenth Century

For many centuries in Ireland, as in other countries throughout the world, flax has been grown, spun by women into yarn, and woven by men into linen cloth. Before cotton became so popular less than two centuries ago, the commonest textiles were linen and wool. Woollens were usually warmer and heavier than linens but until cotton was widely adopted people preferred linen next to their skin for shirts and shifts. Because linen is very strong and long-lasting, whitens well, and does not absorb dirt easily, it was used for pillow-cases and sheets (bed-linens) and for table-cloths and napkins (table-linens). In Ireland however, linens had been traditionally woven on a narrow loom about twenty-four inches wide, easily worked by one man with a helper who wound the yarn for the shuttle. This cloth was coarse in quality and cheap and throughout Ireland in the eighteenth century it was called bandle linen. It satisfied the needs of the ordinary folk who bought cloth in the country markets but wealthier people who wanted finer or broader linens bought either Dutch or German cloth.

It is not likely that an important linen industry would have grown up in Ireland of its own accord because there was not sufficient demand in Ireland for fine linens to encourage many weavers to start making them. In the late seventeenth century, however, among the many thousands of families who emigrated from Britain to Ulster hoping to rent land cheaply, there were skilled weavers. They knew that for very many years considerable quantities of yarn made by the Irish in Ulster had been sold in Manchester. The best of these weavers were able to make cloth fit for sale in the London market and when the British government in 1696 removed the tax on plain linens from Ireland many English dealers began to buy Ulster cloth because it was cheaper than the Dutch and German linens. Since it continued to sell very well more weavers throughout Ulster began to weave for the London market and the industry spread to places as far apart as Strabane, Antrim, and Monaghan before 1710.

The weavers and those who were engaged in the finishing of the linens for the market may also have learned something about their trades from a colony of Huguenots (French Protestants) whom Louis Crommelin brought to Lisburn in 1698. They were heavily financed by the Irish government. The original colony was probably scattered by the great fire which destroyed Lisburn in 1707 for after that date we find few Huguenots of importance in the linen industry. Crommelin's claim that he had established the industry was not contradicted because people had to admit that the great surge forward by the industry occurred after his arrival. They overlooked the fact that Crommelin specialised in fine linens while the London merchants were already buying 'other sorts . . . . . made in the North of Ireland, some yard wide, some three-quarters, and some half-ell [one ell = 45 inches] which are of great use for shirts and wear very white and very strong.'

From pamphlet, *The merchant's warehouse laid open*, published in London 1696 (quoted in *Ulster Journal of Archaeology*, 1st series, III (1855), p.198).

AN

ESSAY

Towards the Improving of the

Hempen and Flaxen

MANUFACTURES

IN THE

KINGDOM

OF

IRELAND.

By *Louis Crommelin* Overſeer of the Royal
Linnen Manufacture of that Kingdom.

D V B L I N :

Printed by *Andrew Crook* Printer to the Queen s moſt
Excellent Majeſty, on the *Blind Key.* 1705.

Title page of the first book published
about the methods and techniques
employed in the linen industry in
Ireland. *(London University Library)*

IHI
1708

THE YEAR ABOUE THIS HOUSE ERECTED
THIS TOWN WAS BURNT Ỹ YEAR BEFORE
PEOPLE THEREIN MAY BE DIRECTED
GOD HATH JUDGMENTS STILL IN STORE
AND THAT THEY DO NOT HIM PROVOKE
TO GIVE TO THEM A SECOND STROKE
THE BUILDER ALSO DOTH DESIRE
AT EXPIRATION OF HIS LEASE
THE LANDLORD LIVING AT THAT TIME
MAY THINK UPON THE BUILDERS CASE

Tablet on the wall of the old Assembly Rooms in Lisburn recording the great fire of 1707. (Lisburn Museum)

So the rapid rise of the industry must really have been due instead to the English decision to remove the duties on Irish linens.

The governments in both London and Dublin were anxious to encourage the linen industry and so in 1711 the Linen Board was established in Ireland to regulate and subsidise the growing industry. Until it was abolished in 1828 the Linen Board did its best to control the development of the industry. It was composed of seventy-two trustees, eighteen from each of the four provinces, all either bishops, nobility, or gentry. The Linen Board tried with some success to encourage the industry by granting money to establish bleachgreens, by spreading the knowledge of new methods and inventions and by awarding prizes for outstanding work by spinners, weavers, or bleachers, In the industry's early years the interest of the Board was valuable because the trustees were influential in Parliament. Few of them, however, knew

3

anything about the industry and much of the business of the Board was conducted by its permanent officials. As the structure of the trade became more complicated many men in the linen business found the Board and its officials more of a hindrance than a help.

Even if the Linen Board had been efficient the linen industry might not have grown, for the success of the linen industry in the eighteenth century depended entirely on the steadily rising demand from England for cheap cloth. The weavers in Ulster could make good cloth cheaper than those of any other country supplying Britain because at first food prices and rents were much lower in Ulster while Irish linens did not have to pay customs duties to enter England. Another important advantage to the industry, especially in the early stages, was the ability of the Dublin merchants to finance the trade with England. The northern linen-drapers needed cash to buy cloth from the weavers and for a long time many of them could not afford to wait for their money until the cloth was sold in England. Therefore for almost a century they carried most of the cloth they made to Dublin and sold it to Dublin factors in the Linen Hall. It was these Dublin merchants who sold the cloth in London.

As the English demand for cloth increased the Ulster linen-drapers found that they had to attend more markets to purchase enough webs

Map of the area around the Linen Hall in Dublin showing the streets named after Ulster linen towns. *(Ordnance Survey)*

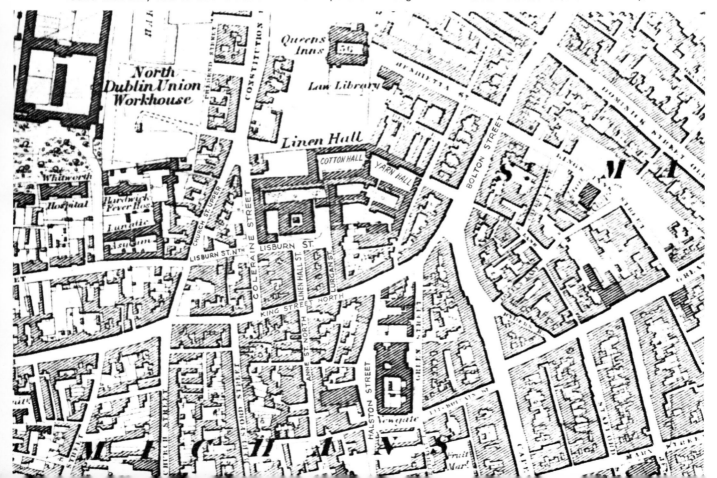

from the weavers but the wealthy linen-drapers could not afford to go to every small town and they concentrated on those towns which had established special linen markets. So both linen and yarn had to be brought by pack-horse or cart to the big markets by dealers who travelled round the small towns and villages in west Ulster and north Connaught. The dealers in yarn were known as *yarn-jobbers* or sometimes as *grey merchants.* Those who bought and sold webs of linen were known as *keelmen.*

The Linen Board tried to expand the linen industry throughout the rest of Ireland. In 1736 they persuaded a Huguenot named De Joncourt to set up a *manufactory* for weaving *cambric* in Dundalk. It is said that this company introduced the weaving of cambrics into Ireland. The manufactory survived for more than twenty years and its success stimulated the Linen Board to sponsor similar enterprises elsewhere. The best-known were those of the Smith family in Waterford, Thomas Adderley at Innishannon and Sir Richard Cox at Dunmanaway (both in County Cork), and William Bryan at Leixlip in County Kildare.

The success of these enterprises was limited by their need to import and depend on Northern techniques, weavers, and bleachers. It was

Gillespie R., and O'Sullivan, H., eds., *The Borderlands: essays on the history of the Ulster-Leinster border* (Belfast, 1989).

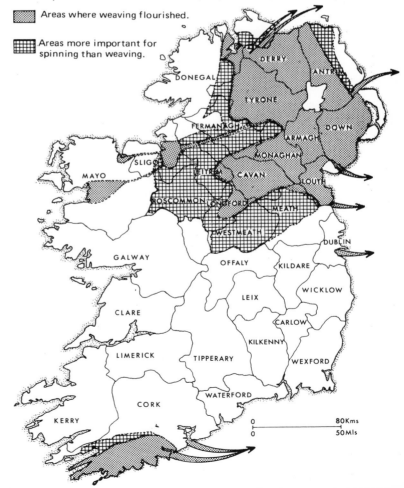

Areas where weaving flourished.

Areas more important for spinning than weaving.

Map to show the extent of the commercial linen handloom weaving industry at its peak about 1810.

5

soon realised that a better solution to the problem would be to attract into the trade those traditional bandle linen-weavers by giving prizes or premiums for the cloths best suited to the English market, and to those drapers who would buy most of them. At first the scheme was successful and many landlords subscribed to further prizes. But when there was a slump in the linen trade in 1773 many of the weavers were unable to sell their cloth and went back to weaving bandle linens: they knew that they could sell them locally. Thus the 1773 crisis marked the end of the attempt to commercialise linen-weaving on a country-wide scale. The southern part of County Cork was able to keep a footing in the English market by supplying very cheap cloth direct to England through the port of Cork. In Drogheda and County Louth the large manufactories continued to be successful. The weaving industry actually increased in Counties Mayo and Sligo in the last few years of the eighteenth century. This may have been because there was no sizeable local market for bandle linens while there was continual demand for more coarse cloth from the Ulster drapers. This rising demand is certainly indicated by a study of the tables showing the amounts of money paid annually in the brown linen markets of the province of Ulster in 1783, 1803, 1816 and 1820 (see pages 79-81). These show that the markets in the west and south of Ulster were growing more rapidly than those in the east between 1783 and 1803.

In Ulster the linen trade continued to expand. The linen-drapers needed more cloth. To weave it more looms were required and more weavers. Many poor people, however, were too poor to afford even the small amount of capital needed to buy and maintain looms, and to purchase yarn, and so they were often glad to get work from a wealthier weaver. The wealthier weavers were usually referred to as manufacturers and by 1800 they comprised the majority of those weavers who actually bought yarn and sold webs of linen in the markets. The manufacturer rented out cottages with small plots of potato ground, known as cottakes, to the cottier-weavers, and often received payment in linen. The number of cottier-weavers grew very rapidly because weaving gave them a basic income and the potato supported them and their families. They were on the whole, as one might expect, very poor.

Sir Charles Coote wrote this account of the situation in County Cavan in 1802:

This middleman is generally a manufacturer of linen who employs journeymen. He rents perhaps ten or fifteen acres of land at from fifteen to thirty shillings per acre, according to the quality of the land and the number of cottages erected on it. This he divides into so many parts as he has capital to employ journeymen. He sets a rood of ground for fifty shillings: his [the tenant's] tenure is called a dry cot-take; if he has grass for a cow he pays for it, from one or two guineas additional, which is termed a wet cot-take.

Statistical Survey ... County Cavan, (1802), pp.41–2.

Yet the closing years of the eighteenth century were the 'Golden Age' of the domestic industry for many Ulster families. All the members of the family could be employed. Children from an early age learned to spin and wind yarn with their mothers and grown sisters while the young men wove with their fathers. The father by virtue of his natural authority and his experience in the trade, attended the markets to buy yarn and to sell the webs. There was no need for everyone to lose a day's pay especially in a busy period when linen prices were high. The family which had a surplus of yarn took a journeyman who lodged with the family and was paid a quarter of the value of what he wove. Many writers commented on the prosperity of the weavers about 1800. Of County Armagh Sir Charles Coote wrote:

The number of looms exceeds the number of houses, as most houses have two or three looms, and frequently they are all at work, when the demand for linens is brisk, at which time many new looms are made, so that we may fairly assert that the number of looms is increasing: flax land being in great demand and of higher value, is a proof there is no diminution in the trade.

Statistical Survey ... County Armagh, (1804), p.269.

John McEvoy added about County Tyrone:

Statistical Survey ... County Tyrone, (1804), p.135.

Common labourers, who were not much in the habit of weaving some years ago, generally work out two or three yards of linen at night in the winter time, after the common day's labour is over.

Marketing in the Eighteenth Century

Throughout the eighteenth century most of the brown (unbleached) linens woven in Ulster were sold in the brown linen markets by weavers to linen-drapers. These linen-drapers were often bleachers (or their agents) who were buying the cloth for their bleaching-greens. When the cloth was bleached the bleachers either took it to the white linen halls in Dublin or Belfast (after 1782) or sent it off in boxes to factors in London.

In the early years of the eighteenth century the linen had often been sold with cattle and provisions in the customary fairs and markets. As the trade increased, however, markets were established throughout Ulster specifically for the sale of linens. Therefore about 1760 the linen-drapers declared in advertisements in the *Belfast News-Letter* that they would no longer attend the country fairs because 'the selling of linen in fairs is not only become unnecessary but highly inconvenient and troublesome' . . . . since 'the buyers and sellers of brown linens do often suffer inconveniences and loss for want of accommodations in country fairs'. They complained that 'by means of the hurry and confusion to which they [the markets] are liable several kinds of fraud and roguery have often been successfully practised'.

Conrad Gill in *The Rise of the Irish Linen Industry* gives a very clear picture of the conduct of the public markets:

The draper seldom had a chance to examine the goods at all adequately before buying them. Standing on his stone or at his stall in the open market he was confronted with a crowd of buyers who passed quickly before him, allowing him time for only a glance at their webs. Each buyer had to buy in this way, within one or two hours, some dozens of pieces from as many weavers. The pieces were nearly always rolled up tightly and tied at the ends so that the buyers could see no more than

Page from the export book of James Ferguson, a Belfast linen-draper, showing how in 1771 he calculated his costs and profit on a box of linens sent by ship to his London agents (PRONI D.468).

Banbridge linen market about 1780. Many market houses were built with such open arches to provide shelter for buyers and sellers. The weavers are holding up their webs to attract the notice of the linen-drapers. Note the inn sign of The Bunch of Grapes.
(*Hincks engraving*)

Conrad Gill, *The Rise of the Irish Linen Industry*, (1925), p.69.

the *selvage* and about a yard of cloth on the outside of the roll. It was regularly contrived that this exposed 'lap-yard' should be the best part of the piece. The weaver, when his bargain was struck, would carry his cloth to the draper's warehouse, or more commonly to a room in an inn hired for the purpose, and there when the market was over the draper would measure the cloth, but necessarily with such haste that he could not thoroughly test the quality. Thus linen sold in the northern markets was never properly examined until it was opened out for bleaching, and often it was not inspected at all.

This account of a linen market gives the impression that the linen-draper was at the mercy of the weaver, but this was by no means the case. The weaver usually named the price he wanted per yard which was really a claim for the quality of the cloth. Then followed a few moments of bargaining or haggling. If the weaver was not satisfied with the price the draper offered, he took his web round the other drapers in the market until he finally sold it. When the weaver agreed on a price with a draper, the draper's clerk wrote his master's name on the piece with the price per yard and handed it back to the weaver. When the market

Gold and silver coins (mainly Spanish and Portuguese) which were used in Ireland throughout much of the eighteenth century. The small pair of scales was carried about in a pocket case to check whether the coins were up to their correct weights. *(Ulster Museum)*

ended the draper went off to his inn and there in a room the pieces were measured and the money paid out in cash (for the weavers would not risk taking banknotes or bills of exchange). The weaver had to give the draper a penny off the price towards payment for the room in the inn.

The customs of the market were well understood but often broken. An advertisement in the *Belfast News-Letter* of 24 January 1766 illustrates how seriously the linen-drapers viewed the bargain struck in the market.

Notice is hereby given for the good of the linen trade that on Friday the 10th instant in the market of Lurgan Mr. James McCalpin of Belfast, linen-draper, bought a piece of brown linen cloth from Henry Smith of Lurgan and wrote his name thereon and the price thereof as usual. And that afterwards on the same day and in the same open market the same piece of cloth was again produced for sale to the said Mr. McCalpin with marks defaced by one McAnulty near Lurgan; which the said Mr. Mc

THE noted Inn, in the town of Lurgan, formerly known by the sign of the Bear, but now the Spread Eagle, is opened by Thomas Overend, who takes this opportunity to inform his friends and the publick, that he has laid in choice clarret, Lisbon, and best white wines, two year old mead, plain brandy and rum, double rum, cherry brandy, rasberry ditto: He likewise has brewed a large stock of wholesom ale and beer: He has likewise exceeding good stabling, and standing for thirty horses; and has laid in a large quantity of dry land hay, and has now by him some choice old oats; and as he is a beginner, he will take the utmost care to pleafe both his friends and the publick, and hopes by his affiduity to merit their good esteem.

N. B. He defigns to have always by him the best kind of Carinford Orfters during the feason.

Advertisement for the Sign of the Spread
Eagle, Lurgan in 1762. 24 September 1762
(Belfast News-Letter)

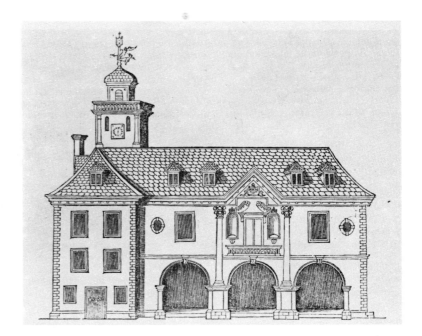

Londonderry market house built in 1692.
*(Colby, Ordnance Survey of the County
Londonderry, vol. 1)*

Calpin detected and seized the said McAnulty and brought him before a magistrate there, when it appeared that the said web was the property of of a certain manufacturer in Lurgan.

This criminal practice, as it is a prevailing one and no particular means pointed out by the linen laws for punishment, the said Mr. McCalpin with the approbation of the said magistrate recommended the premises and submitted the penalty to be inflicted for the said offence to the gentlemen of the Lurgan club partly consisting of linen-drapers, who determined that the offender (being the manufacturer) should pay the sum of £3 to be distributed among the poor of the said town and parish of Lurgan; which good example is thus made known as worthy an imitation in cases of this kind that frequently happen.

The linen-draper would have been happy to buy his cloth regularly from those weavers who had sold him good webs in the past, but throughout the late eighteenth century most of the weavers were independent and able to go round the market looking for the best price they could get for their webs. The market-book of Thomas Greer of Dungannon in 1758-9 shows that even in his home market at Dungannon he bought 559 pieces from 329 weavers, of whom 233 sold to him on only one occasion and 64 on two occasions. In these circumstances Thomas Greer had to do the best he could. The price he would offer for a web would depend on the number of webs he needed for his bleach-green and the price other drapers were offering. He would try to find out what the prospects were like for future markets, hoping to put off buying until the price fell: if not all of the other drapers were going to attend he would be able to buy his cloth more cheaply.

The linen-drapers by refusing to buy might push down the price of the webs hoping that the weavers would be glad to sell their webs cheaply instead of taking them back home and keeping them there until the next market. On the other hand it was obviously an advantage to the weaver if he was able to wait until he could get a good price and not in a great hurry to sell. Therefore dealers were prepared to buy linens from the country people in their homes or even on their way to market in order to sell for a higher price and so make a good profit. This was why we find Thomas Greer buying cloth from the same person in more than one market. Of those he dealt with in Dungannon he purchased from three in Moneymore (County Londonderry), fourteen in Stewartstown and nine in Caledon (both in County Tyrone), six in Armagh city and two in Monaghan town. He bought from four in three separate markets.

These dealers were usually known as jobbers. Although their business reputations were sometimes shady they played a vital role in bringing cloth to the markets. A good description of the range of their activities was written by James Corry, the Secretary of the Linen Board, in 1816. He distinguished several kinds of jobbers:

(1)   The jobber who buys at a market one day and sells at another market the following day. To this species of jobbing, though contrary to law, the regular buyers do not anywhere object, for it is a convenience to them, they say, to have those under-agents bring linens from distant markets, to which they would not think it worth the

J. Horner, *The linen trade of Europe during the spinning wheel era* (1920), pp.149–50 quoting Corry's report.

12

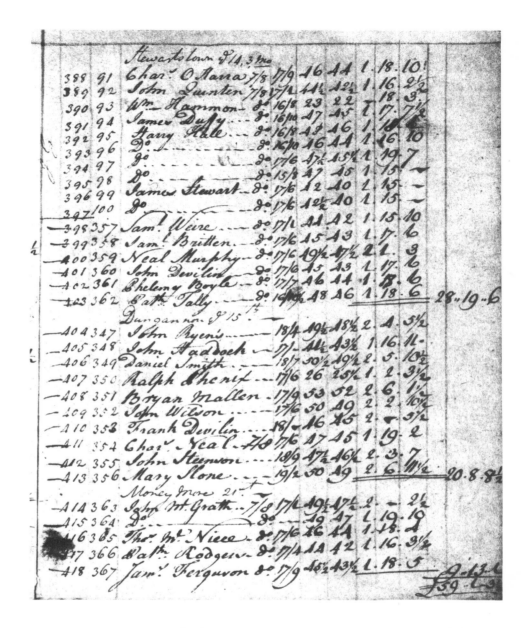

Page from the market book of the Dungannon (County Tyrone) linen draper Thomas Greer in 1759 showing how he and his men attended the local linen markets to purchase cloth from the weavers. Note that the names of the weavers are English, Irish and Scottish (PRONI T.1127/4).

trouble of going to buy. Such jobbers they almost consider fair traders, because they take their chance of the rise or fall of markets.

(2)   The jobber who buys in a market one day and sells in the same market on a subsequent day. This is a class of jobbers more objectionable, though they must take their chance in the market.

(3)   The jobber who buys and sells in the same market on the same day. This is the worst of all kinds of jobbing. The jobber in this case is a

Armagh market place in 1810.
(Armagh Museum)

A jobber bringing cloth to a market.

kind of middle-man who cheats the poor weaver of a fair price and the buyer of his profit, and gets rich on the industry of both. If the first buying in this case is before market hour, the offence should perhaps be called forestalling.

There is a fourth description of unfair dealing which takes place in the market, and which cannot be called jobbing, nor perhaps forestalling, and yet is not less objectionable than either. It is this:

(4)   The weaver brings his webs to the bench of the buyer before market hour, submits them to his inspection, and has an arrangement with him as to which he shall buy, before the market begins. This is an offence which cheats the regular buyer of the advantage of open market; it is one in which the purchaser who so deals is as much to blame as the weaver; but it is only practised by under-agents or commissioners, as they call them, not by bleachers or principal buyers. All these irregularities are found to exist more or less in the market of Dungannon.

As the eighteenth century wore on another character who appeared more often in the linen markets was the small manufacturer. It is likely that the first of this class sold only the linen produced by their sons and by any journeyman they employed when the price of linen was high. Their success encouraged many farmer-weavers, especially in the poorer

14

areas, to employ as journeymen poor men who paid their rent to the farmer-weaver in work. This was, in a sense, an early form of the putting-out system (see the chapter on the Development of the Putting-out System).

As the demand for cloth grew, landowners were encouraged to establish or revive linen markets in their towns because they knew the industry would bring prosperity to the town (e.g. Ballyclare, Bally-money, and Ahoghill in County Antrim; Portadown and Markethill in County Armagh; Hillsborough in County Down; and Bellaghy in County Londonderry). They offered special facilities to the linen-drapers and one landlord even offered to entertain the linen-drapers who attended the market in his town. The greatly increased number of markets in the 1750s strengthened the bargaining position of the linen-drapers still further and enabled them to stipulate the terms on which they would attend the markets. These they set out in an advertisement in the *Belfast News-Letter* of 1 September 1758.

The majority of the linen-drapers who attend the markets of Belfast, Lisburn, Lurgan, Newry, Loughbrickland, Rathfriland, Banbridge, Dromore, Hillsborough, Richhill, Armagh, Tandragee, Loughgall, Dungannon, Caledon, and Monaghan, having had several meetings in order to fix upon some new regulations for the better improvement of the brown linen markets, have unanimously agreed to the following resolutions.
Resolved, that after the first day of October next, we will return all brown linens bought by us in any of the markets, that exceed twenty-five yards the single piece or fifty yards the double piece.
Resolved, that after the said first day of October, we are determined to have one yard to the single piece and two yards to the double piece on all brown linens bought by us in any of the aforesaid markets.
And in order to make a sufficient recompense to the sellers of brown linens for said yard, and to prevent the many idle disputes arising between buyer and seller at the time of measuring, we recommend it to the magistrates of said towns to have all brown cloth yards cut to thirty-six inches.
And we do hereby give the public notice that after the said first of October we are determined to put the above resolutions into execution.
All those who approve of said resolutions, are desired to attend at Loughbrickland, Armagh, or Monaghan, on Tuesday the third day of October next.

The evidence we have suggests that only in Lurgan market were these resolutions quietly adopted and so the drapers began to look to Parliament and the Linen Board to enforce legislation already on the statute book. The Linen Board in 1733 had appointed lappers to inspect the brown linen cloths when they were brought for sale to the markets but there had been no serious attempt to enforce the act for many years as the linen-drapers were prepared to put up with the faults in the system. Another act of 1745 had ordained that when linen cloth was brought to the market it should not be tied up in rolls but should be made up in open folds so that any part of the web might be

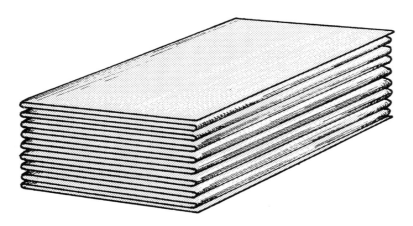

Lapped cloth. Cloth folded in this way could easily be opened by the linen-draper to inspect every fold.

examined. This act also had been disregarded.

In the late 1750s, even the linen-drapers found that they could no longer afford to overlook the problem of badly woven cloth as there were many complaints from English merchants and a serious danger of Irish linen losing its reputation in the English market. Shortly before 1760 one firm complained that it had just lost £1,000 through the return of cloth that had been badly woven. The linen-drapers decided to persuade Parliament and the Linen Board to enforce a scheme of inspection based on the acts of 1733 and 1745. The Linen Board decided to appoint brown-sealmasters and re-issued instructions that every web of brown (unbleached) linen which they stamped had to be of good and even quality; that no cloth was to be sealed during the market (inspection had to be completed before the market began); that the sealmaster might charge one penny for each piece that he sealed; and that the various sorts of cloth had to be made according to the conditions laid down in the 1745 act.

The Northern weavers let their opposition to the bill be known. They were convinced that the drapers were trying to use the force of law to gain control of the industry and they met to plan resistance. When the law was to be enforced for the first time in Lisburn market on 18 May 1762 a large body of weavers marched throughout the town, beating up drapers and damaging property. So many people disapproved of this conduct that the rioters found themselves isolated and

Linen seals used to stamp linens with the name of the weaver or bleacher.
(H.D. Gribbon and Ulster Museum)

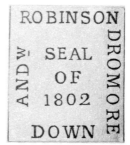

21 and 22 Geo. III c.35.

John Nevill, *Seasonable remarks on the linen trade of Ireland* (1783) p.41 (Linenhall Library N.4523).

powerless when Lord Hillsborough introduced the new system of brown seals into Lisburn market. The system of sealing brown linens was widely accepted and Parliament was so encouraged that it passed an act in 1764 which recognised the new system. But the brown seals were given not to the linen-drapers or their agents, nor to government inspectors, but more often than not to the weavers themselves so that twenty years later it was said that there was 'hardly a weaver in the north of Ireland but in time became a sealmaster'.

The struggle between the linen-drapers and the weavers slept for almost twenty years but in 1782 it took a new twist. The drapers had been consulted about a new Linen Bill which they expected would tighten up the administration of the 1764 act against the frauds of the brown-sealmasters. Instead, when the bill was announced they found that they as bleachers would be held responsible and punished for dealing in poor quality cloth. The existing seals were to be withdrawn and they were to be given new seals and become white-sealmasters on condition that they would obey the Linen Board's regulations. Each of them was to swear:

I will not knowingly seal or stamp, or suffer to be sealed or stamped with my seal, any linen that is mildewed, rotten, unmerchantable, or fraudulently made up, bleached or whitened, or stamp or mark, or suffer to be stamped or marked, any false length or breadth thereon.

The Northern linen-drapers were very angry. As one of them argued:

There are many drapers who, by a steady attention, skill and care, have got their names into such repute as to be able to sell any quantity of goods, from their fair character; now by taking the oath (to seal all such linens as are merchantable which may be brought to them) [they] would be throwing away in a moment what took them years to acquire.

Very quickly the drapers united and compelled the Linen Board to withdraw the proposed scheme. But the row had more serious consequences because the Northern drapers blamed the Dublin factors for causing the crisis and various groups of drapers passed resolutions which resulted in the establishment of white linen halls in Newry (1783) and

Belfast (1785). Dublin lost its role as the great market for white linens but this was not so much the result of competition from the Belfast and Newry white linen halls as a consequence of a great change in the marketing of linens. Even the new Northern white linen halls were not a success because the individual drapers were now wealthy enough to be capable of dealing directly with the English market and so they did not need to sell their cloth through the white linen halls.

The draper and the bleacher now played the key roles in marketing Irish linens in Britain. It would be more accurate to talk about the draper-bleacher since the bleacher or his employees acted as drapers to purchase webs for the bleachgreen. A popular song of the period praising the County Monaghan linen-draper, Hugh Jackson of Ballybay, gives this description of his business:

> His mill, kilns and barns, they cut a great show,
> His cloths to the North and the City do go,
> For bleaching and lapping he exceeds them all,
> And his cloth first approved of at the Linen Hall.

An idea of the business of an important bleacher-draper can be gained from a letter written by Thomas Greer in 1782 to his English partners:

Hillmount bleachgreen near Cullybackey (County Antrim) established in the early eighteenth century. *(Ulster Museum)*

Robin Morton, *Folksongs sung in Ulster* (1970).

PRONI D. 1044/661.
I think you may know that every piece of brown linen bought by Benjamin Greer is received here, examined, measured, entered into the proper books, marked for bleaching, and afterwards sent to the green; that every time linens are sorted at New Hambro [the name of his bleachgreen] I or my son or Thomas Boardman attends there, sorts and invoices them; that I also hold an account with John Greer, supply him with cash for paying bleachers and labourers, examine all his disbursements, the bleachers' accounts, etc., etc., and that you also consider me accountable for him. I think that you must know that some trouble and expense attends the procuring bleaching stuffs such as going or sending one of my family to Newry to purchase on the best terms and choose the best quality, receiving them at Moy or Coalisland [by canal], getting them stored or sent properly to the green, not to speak of the risk of loss on non-entries of disbursements; in short were I to particularise the whole with the many accounts, letter-writing, bill-drawing, the trouble of procuring casks, the sum I get for it is not adequate . . . .

PRONI D. 562/1270 (see also p.76).
Many of these bleachers became wealthy in the second half of the eighteenth century. It was reckoned, for example, that in 1795 there were in County Armagh 51 bleachyards whitening 162,500 pieces of cloth which had cost the bleachers about £270,000. One of the richest linen-drapers in the county was the Quaker Thomas Christy of Moyallen who died in the spring of 1780. He left to his son-in-law a bleachgreen capable of finishing 8,000 pieces annually with many pieces of property throughout Ulster; between two of his grandsons he divided money and 6,000 acres in North Carolina; and to each of five grand-daughters he gave £2,000. It was the wealth of such men as Thomas Christy and his successors which saved the Ulster linen industry in the early nineteenth century for they helped to build first the big spinning mills and later the weaving factories.

PRONI T. 1976/1.
In the late eighteenth century, however, the bleacher-draper was not the only dealer who marketed Irish linens in England. He did business with important merchants in England and so he had to guarantee the quality of the cloth and its finish. Thus there was also scope for a class of pedlars known as *keelmen* who were active buyers in the markets, finished their cloth to much lower standards than the Linen Board stipulated, and travelled through England to sell them at a lower price than other Irish linens. An observer in Armagh market in 1821 estimated that they comprised 60 of the 170 buyers there and remarked about them:

The keelmen were so-called from the first persons who got into the trade. Being very illiterate and unable to write in ordinary characters, they marked on each piece of linen the price at which it was bought with keel, that is iron ore which makes a red mark that will not rub out. The buyers were originally a peculiar race of travelling pedlars who went over to England to retail linens which, seventy years ago, they generally bought from the bleachers. But now they buy them in the brown market, half bleach them with lime in a corner of one of their fields, get them a few hours beetling in a neighbouring bleachfield and when ready

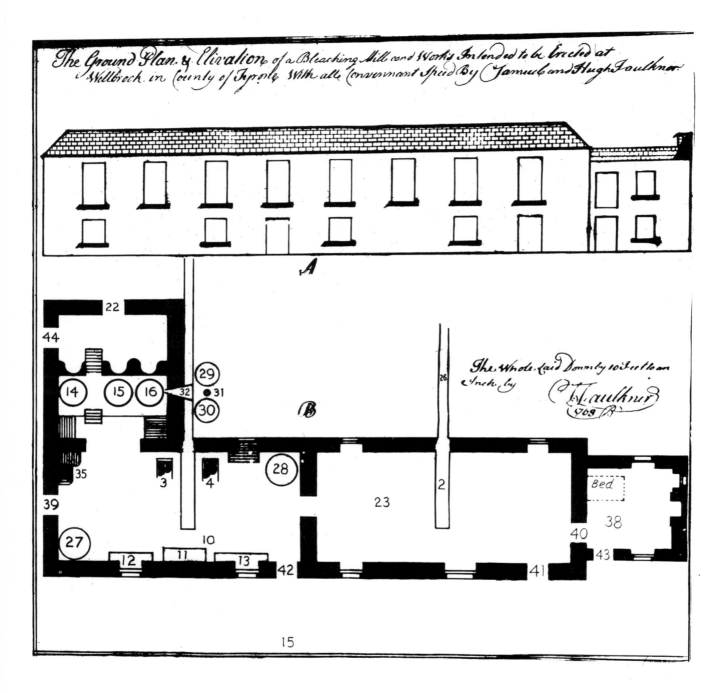

The Ground Plan & Elevation of a Bleaching Mill and Works Intended to be Erected at Wellbrook in County of Tyrone With all Convenient Speed By Samuel and Hugh Faulkner.

The Whole Laid Down by 10 Feet to an Inch by CFaulkner 1768

Kirk of Keady's comment in J. Corry, *Report on the measuring and stamping of brown linen sold in public market* (Dublin, 1822), Appendix, 174–5.

KEY

No. 1.	The grate watter wheel which works two wash mills turns two cranks which cranks works 4 payr of rubb boards and 2 drawing engins for the us of the rubb boards.
No. 2.	The grate watter wheel which works two wash mills turns two with their travses each engin contains thirty six beetels.
3 & 4	The sate of the two washmills.
5 : 6 : 7 : 8	The sate of the cogg wheels and cranks that drives the four payr of rubb boards.
9 : 10	The sate of the drawing engins.
11	A large box that receives ye linen after being rubbed from the drawing engins.
12 : 13	Two large tabels for soping the linens on before it gos into the rubb boards.
14 : 15 : 16	Three large furnises capable of boyling 100 pieces of linen each.
17 : 18 : 19	The fire plases to the furnises.
20	The steps up to the furnises.
21	A door and steps from furnises down to ye fires.
22	A large window to which the turf is wheeld and empit down to the fire plases.
23 : 24	The state of the beetling engins.
25	The watter which works the washmills and rubb boards 22 feet falls and a grate plenty at the driest seasons.
26	The watter which works the beetling engins. This is intirely exelant spring water and at full sufficient to serve this wheel at all seasons and from the hight of 30 feet which it rises to heare can be very reddely conved to all the other parts of the works to serve the head stocks boylers sour keves etc.
27 : 28	Two large sour keves to contain 100 pieces of linen.
29 : 30	Two large kelp keves.
31	A pump which supleys the two kelp keves with soft water from the iron of ye watter wheels.
32	A large iron which recives the fine lees from the kelp keves and conves it to the furneises.
33 : 34	Racks to drain the linen after boyling.
35 : 36	Racks to drain the linen after washing in ye mills.
37	A door from the rubboards into ye engin house.
38	The laping room clarks office ye store room under it.
39	The principle doore from the works into ye green.
40	A door from ye drying loft into ye lapping room.
41 : 2 : 3 : 4	Doors in to diffrant parts of the workes.

This is to be built on a plott of ground containing ten acres held by lease of lives renewable for ever in county of Tyrone and Barony of Dungannon Mannor of Orator and parish of Killdress.

A beetling mill (for finishing linens during the bleaching) near Wellbrook today, as restored by the National Trust.

Ground plan and elevation of Wellbrook bleaching mill near Cookstown (County Tyrone), 1762. PRONI T.1617/5/2.

go with them to England, retail them there, and return to buy again. From their mode of living and the exchange of English bills, they have generally made money; and so great is this trade just now that I am certain they buy in Armagh market alone from 1,500 to 1,700 pieces weekly. They can now pretty generally read and write though to this day it is not uncommon to see some of them putting on his hieroglyphics with keel as formerly.

Among the papers in the Public Record Office there is a copy of a diary kept by an unknown young man who went with a friend, James Patterson, to sell linens on commission in Liverpool in December 1778. For each piece of linen that he sold at a price set by its owner he received payment as commission. If he managed to make a better bargain with the buyer then the profit was his. The following extracts from the diary show how he sold his linens.

Thursday the 10th
We tried to sell some cloth and I sold a piece to the Reverend Mr Kitchin near the Theatre. Same night he sent a girl to my lodgings to desire me to send him his money or another web for the one he had got was holed, upon which I promised to go to his house next day at 9 o'clock and if it had any holes that was not exposed to sight I would take it back again.

Friday the 11th
After I got breakfast I went to Mr Kitchin's and took some more cloth with me and after some conversation I took the web and gave him another for it which [was] ¾d less per yard. And afterwards I sold the

22

same piece to another at 2d per yard more and likewise one of Mr Auld's at 2 shillings valued to me at 23d per yard. [Webs were either 25 or 50 yards long according to the kind of linen.]

Wednesday the 16th

In the morning we went to look at some hardware which a man wanted to barter to [= for] linen but could not deal with him and then we went to a gentleman's house at No. 11 in Cleton Square and James Patterson bartered one piece of his own and one of mine to a watch.

PRONI T. 1763.

Extract from the diary of a man selling linens on commission in Liverpool in 1778. (PRONI T.1763)

23

The Weavers in the Eighteenth Century

Visitors to Ireland were surprised to find that the majority of the weavers in Ulster lived not in towns but in the countryside. They felt that weavers should be gathered into towns for the convenience of the industry and so that the countryside might once more be cultivated by farmers according to the best methods instead of the hand-to-mouth practices of the weavers on their small farms. The weaver, however, held a different point of view. He knew from bitter experience that food prices could fluctuate from week to week and that if there was a depression in the trade there would be a poor price for his cloth. The food he could grow on his small farm would save him when the price of oatmeal and potatoes got too high in the markets. When he went to market to sell his web he would not have to take any price the draper cared to offer but he would be able to bargain as well as his neighbour.

Yet the weaver did not wish to live too far away from the market where he sold his webs and bought yarn, provisions, and candles, because he would lose time on the road to the market. Therefore he was prepared to pay a high rent to obtain a holding close to a good market town. As an agent wrote to a landlord in 1764: 'The manufacturers of brown linen in the neighbourhood of Waringstown and Lurgan [County Armagh], whose stock is barely sufficient to keep their looms in work and support their families, will give twenty shillings or a guinea per acre for a small farm with a convenient house thereon, and even at that price find it difficult to get proper accommodation.' Observers commented that the weaver was paying for 'his accommodation'. Sir Charles Coote described the whole situation neatly and accurately: 'Agriculture is a secondary motive; it is merely pursued as the means of supply of provision, rather than of trade from which any profit may be gained.'

PRONI T. 1181/1.

Statistical Survey ... County Armagh (1804), p.261.

Tillage farming and weaving did not go well together. A weaver of fine linens had to be careful about his hands because rough hands could snag the cloth while fingers thickened by too much manual labour were clumsy at the loom. He was not dependent on farming for his living and so he did not pay enough attention to it. As long as linen prices were good he did not worry unduly about his crop yields: he could always buy meal and potatoes in the market. He grew some flax which employed the women of the family in spinning yarn for the loom, and some oats and potatoes for their food; a cow or two provided enough milk for the family and for making the butter which his wife churned for the market. It was reckoned that 'a farm of ten acres, after supplying the family with milk, sells one hundredweight of butter *each year;* two acres keeps the two cows'. A farm of this size usually also supported a horse (something of a status symbol), a pig and a few poultry.

E. Wakefield, *An account of Ireland* (Dublin, 1812), note on p.364.

Because he could make more money from his cloth than even quite substantial farmers from their farms alone the weaver of fine linens was able to outbid them for the small-holding he wanted. The weaver of coarse linens was not so fortunate except when the price of linen was exceptionally high. Usually he leased a cottage and a garden and some-times 'a cow's grass' from a wealthier tenant farmer whom he would have to pay in money, in cloth, or in farm-work during springtime and harvest. This meant that when the market prices for both linen and grain were good the farmer was saved from having to pay a high wage to hire agricultural labourers. In Cavan and Monaghan and other remote areas in Ulster the cottier-weaver often had to depend for his livelihood on tenant-farmers or other weavers to let him a small-holding and provide him with yarn. Because he was completely dependent on this middleman the cottier-weaver either had to weave for him at a fixed rate or pay an exorbitant price for the yarn. Many of these middlemen were merely weavers and yarn-jobbers who had made enough money to secure a situation in life which enabled them to exploit other poor people. The 'yarn jobbers' were notorious money-lenders. In return for a loan the spinner had to give the jobber his yarn as it was spun at a low

Detail from Rocque's map of County Armagh 1760 which illustrates how densely the countryside was populated by linen-weavers. (PRONI D.602).

price. If he dared to dispute the price offered, the jobber would require immediate repayment of the loan and interest.

It is clear, however, that as the linen trade prospered it provided employment for an increasing number of people. Weavers bred up their children to the trade and even quite well-to-do farmers sent their younger sons to learn weaving so that they 'were enabled by proper economy and application in a few years to purchase farms'. Since the weaving of the coarser sorts of cloth did not require much skill many labourers turned to weaving when linen prices were good and farm wages poor.

The linen industry was to a great extent responsible for the rapid growth of the population in the linen country. When a man learned how to weave he was independent and so he could afford to marry. His parents encouraged him to marry and settle down and often provided him with some of their own land for a house and garden. Even if they did not approve his marriage he could follow his own fancy because his wife would probably be a spinner anyway. So prosperity can break down social conventions and enable a man to be independent and to challenge authority. Young children, who were counted as so many mouths to feed on a farm, were an asset in a weaver's home. From an early age they were taught to spin and wind yarn and when boys were strong enough they learned to weave. Therefore no one should be surprised that on the eve of the Great Famine, County Armagh was the most densely populated county in Ireland with 511 persons to the square mile while another seven counties with a density of more than 400 to the square mile included the linen counties of Cavan, Monaghan, Tyrone and Down.

If the rapid growth of the population was a result of the prosperity created by the linen industry it may have happened because the children were better nourished and more likely to survive those diseases which had always carried them off in great numbers. For one thing food supplies became more regular in the second half of the eighteenth century and there were no serious famines with great loss of life as there had been in 1728-29, 1740-41 and 1744-45. Improved roads, new canals, and coastal shipping prevented serious local shortages of oatmeal and potatoes, the staple foods of the people. The northern weavers preferred oatmeal which they believed was a more substantial food but when its price rose above the average many poor people lived entirely upon potatoes and milk. It was said that oatmeal was the bread of the north but from quite early in the century potatoes were the food of the poor. When potatoes ran short towards the end of the spring they suffered some privation until the new crop was ready about August. The better-off weavers, however, were able to afford meat at least once a week and it was commented that many of them had tea for breakfast. The weavers had, too, the produce of their gardens to flavour the food: *champ,* which was merely a mixture of potatoes and onions, was particularly popular. Bacon, herrings, and butter were *kitchen* for they gave a relish to the otherwise plain food. A favourite dish made from oatmeal was *sowans* prepared from the husks of oatmeal. Boiling water

Feb. 1. Buried Matthew Son of John Lavery of Drumnaferry.
3. Buried Susanna Wife of James Macoun of Edenballycoggill.
4. Buried Murthagh Heany from Kilwardlin.
6. Married David Bell and Margaret Parker of Ballymncean.
10. Buried Mary Dau: of Edward & Susanna Nagle of Magheralin.
13. Buried A Child of John Jenkins of Maralin Shoemaker.
14. Buried A Child of Bryan Lavery's from Moyrah Parish.
17. Buried Elizabeth Dau: of widow Conky of Maralin.
18. Buried ——— Dau: of Bryan McIlboy of Drumnaferry.
19. Buried Elinor Dau: of Widow McClatchy of Maralin.
19. Buried Richard Demply of Maralin.
19. Buried Hugh Dales of Dromore.
19. Buried Dmund Lavery from Ballenderry.
20. Buried Jean Dau: of Thomas & Catherine Walker of Dromo & ...
22. Buried Margaret Wife of Knocher Lavery of Benmore.
23. Buried Jean Dau: of Hugh Walker of Tullyard.
23. Buried Margaret Read a poor Woman from the Glebe.
24. Buried Andrew Son of Dan: & Mary Campbell of Dromo & ...
25. Buried Patrick Son of Patrick McKeonan of Lissncan.

Entries for February 1741 in the parish register of Magheralin (County Down) illustrating the severe toll of that month, in that rural weaving parish (PRONI T.679/376).

was poured on the husks in a tub, and the whole well stirred. It was left for five or six days to sour, then strained and boiled until it assumed the consistency of thin porridge. A housewife's reputation depended on the quality of her sowans and her butter.

The prosperity of the weavers was reflected not only in their food but in their housing and their dress. Travellers soon realised when they had entered 'the linen country': the counties of Cavan, Monaghan, Armagh, west Down and east Tyrone. In 1756 the famous evangelist, John Wesley, remarked, 'No sooner did we enter Ulster than we observed the difference. The ground was cultivated just as in England, and the cottages not only neat, but with doors, chimneys and windows.' A more extravagant picture was painted about the same period by Edward Willes, a judge travelling through the country on circuit:

From Dundalk we went to Monaghan. Nothing very remarkable in that

27

journey but from Monaghan quite to Carrickfergus, which is about fifty miles, is the very picture of industry, nor did I ever see in England or Ireland a finer cultivated country. The whole road for the space of fifty miles is, as it were, one continued village of neat cottages, for I believe in the whole space you are never two hundred yards distance from a pretty cabin, and what adds to the beauty is [that] every cabin has a little orchard belonging to it, and spinning or weaving or some branch of the manufacture is going on in every house. 'Tis a fine sight to behold the great number of bleach yards: they look like white patches of unmelted snow in the winter time.

The weavers' cottages which he saw were long, low thatched cottages, well whitewashed against the weather. The houses ranged in value from about £5 to about £40. A proposed model of cottage suggested for Rathfriland in 1764 was sixteen feet wide with a workshop twenty feet long to contain four looms, a kitchen of fourteen feet and a bedroom of sixteen feet. It was reckoned that such a house with a seven-foot side wall, a loft above the workshop and the floor of the workshop sunk three feet to contain the height of the looms, would cost £30 to build. This house must have been built of stone and slate but the majority of weavers lived in much poorer houses. In north Armagh the walls were usually made of mud rough cast with lime but in the hilly country of south Armagh and Monaghan mud walls were practically unknown. On top of the length of the house stretching from gable to gable were laid timbers called *purlins* which carried the thatch roof of wheat straw. These were the houses of which the construction costs were quoted by Young in 1776 at £5 and by Coote in 1802 at £8.

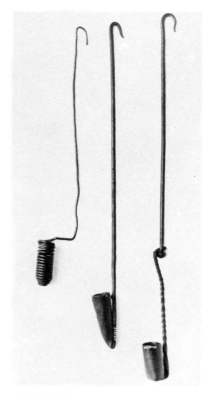

PRONI T. 2368.

Household items typical of a weaver's possessions in eighteenth-century Ulster: piggin and noggin, weavers' candlesticks, butter print, knife box, and turned wooden bowl. (*Armagh Museum*)
Ref nos 70–47, 42–38, 160–58.

28

Spinning wheel. The wheel (a) is driven by the spinner's foot working the treadle (b). By one cord it turns the bobbin (c) on which the thread is wound, and by the other cord (for the wheel has two grooves) it turns the whole spindle (d) on which the semi-circular flyer (e) revolves to control the way the thread (f) is fed by the spinner from the lint on the 'rock' or distaff (g). *(Ulster Folk Museum)*

The weaver's cottage brought from the Lurgan area to the Ulster Folk Museum. All of the house to the left of the front door comprises the workshop which was originally designed for four looms. The man is sitting on the shaft of a linen cart.

It was in the workshops of these houses that the weavers wove the cloth. The weaver grew some of his own flax if he had a small farm, but he often needed to buy more in the market or from a travelling yarn-jobber: scutched flax was usually bought by the hundredweight for the family to spin. If he needed the spun yarn urgently he would buy it in spangles or hanks (four hanks in a spangle of 14,400 yards) but he would prefer to buy it from someone he could trust as there were such wide variations in the quality of yarn that bad yarn could destroy any profit the weaver might have. A good spinner's reputation was recognised throughout the parish and often much further afield. The yarn was generally unbleached, or *green*, when it was purchased, for each weaver had his own special trade secrets in bleaching it and preparing it for the loom.

The weaver's first task was to *tackle* the loom: to set it up for weaving. Each warp thread had to be tied separately to the warp beam and then wound on it. Then each individual warp thread had to be

Mr John McAtasney of the Ulster Folk Museum weaving a damask napkin, using the flying shuttle (a) which he jerks back and forward with the stick in his right hand. His left hand is pulling the beam, which contains the reed, to tighten each thread which the shuttle pulls through, before pushing it away to make the tunnel for the next throw of the shuttle. With his feet he works the treadles (b) to reverse the threads in the heddles (c) and to change the pattern. The shuttle is reloaded with full bobbins (d), beside the empty bobbins (e). The temples (f) keep the woven cloth taut to prevent the shuttle from catching on the border or selvedge. The warp threads (g) are wound on the warp beam (h). The shears (j) are hanging on the post to his right hand.

30

brought forward on the loom and fed first through the small eyes of the *mails* on the *heddles* and then between the teeth of the comb known as the *reed* before being tied to the cloth beam. Since the warp of a web could contain as many as several thousand threads, tackling the loom was a very tedious job which would take at least a week's work, and often much longer.

There is considerable skill and knowledge required for putting up a loom properly, mounting her, and giving her a complete rig. Sometimes the weaver can do this for himself, but often he possesses not the necessary knowledge, nor the way to carry it into practice. And hence, in almost every country district, there are some of clearer heads and readier hands who became a sort of professors in this line . . . .

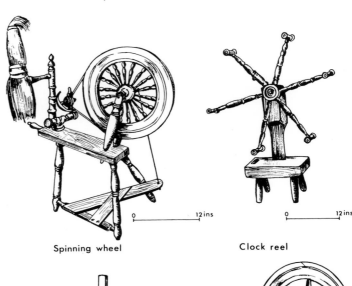

Spinning wheel   Clock reel

Diagram showing the relationship between spinning-wheel, clock reel, swift and pirn winder. The yarn was spun on the spinning wheel. Before it could be sold it had to be wound on a clock reel. The reel was 2½ yards in circumference; 120 threads, each thread being equal to one round, made a cut; 12 cuts made a hank and 4 hanks made a spangle. Yarn was sold by spangles, hanks and cuts.

The weaver who bought the yarn needed the bundles wound on to bobbins, or pirns. The bundle was stretched over the rollers (x) and (y) on the swift, and the thread drawn on to the bobbin (z) by turning the handle of the pirn-winder. (the diagram is based on illustrations taken from the Ulster Museum publication *Spinning Wheels*)

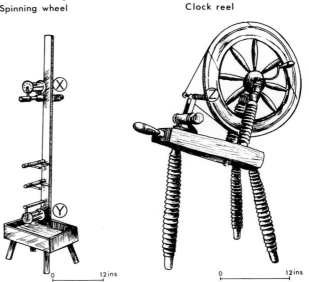

Swift   Pirn winder

31

I went to my loom to see was she in tune,
But from her full soon I was obliged to go;
Neither headles, nor jacks, nor slays were correct,
The spring staves and treadles were all wrong below.

Verse by Peter Burns of Kilwarlin.

When the warp was mounted on the loom the weaver prepared the exposed warp threads in order to make them easier to weave. First he brushed a thin dressing of flour and water into the warp threads and fanned them dry with a wing. Then he rubbed the threads thoroughly with tallow. This treatment made weaving much simpler and gave it a better finish, and the dressing was easily dissolved during the bleaching.

During very hot weather or in frost weavers often complained that the dressing would not stand in the loom but flaked away from the threads. It was very important to maintain a cool temperature and damp atmosphere in the workshop in order to prevent the threads in the loom

Weaver using the hand-shuttle. He had to change hands to throw the shuttle through the 'shed' in the warp threads. He is pulling the beam with his right hand. Note the two bundles of yarn hanging over the loom.
(detail from Hincks engraving)

32

from drying and snapping. This is why the floors of every workshop were composed only of earth. Tying broken threads could be a time-consuming chore and tested a weaver's patience.

When the warp was dressed the weaver needed the *bobbins* of spun yarn for the shuttle. These were prepared by the females and boys of the family who wound the thread on spools called *pirns* from a large revolving frame called a *swift*. The pirns or bobbins were put into the shuttle. Until the end of the eighteenth century the hand shuttle was the only shuttle used in the Irish linen industry: although Kay's 'flying shuttle' was well known and used by the cotton handloom weavers in Belfast it was not applied to linen weaving. 'There was strong prejudice against the flying-shuttle because it was new and because the hand shuttle had done a long time and had made good weavers, far better, it was prophesied, than would ever be made by any other mode whatever.' It may have had to await the invention of the *temples* (by a Dromore man about 1800) a very simple wooden construction designed to keep the width of the cloth fully stretched so that the selvages were not pulled out of shape. By keeping the selvages flat on the loom it prevented them from snagging the shuttle.

The weaver's year was dictated by the seasons since bleaching was considered to be a job for the summer months. It was believed that linens bleaching could be damaged by frost. Bleaching was essential not only to whiten the linen but to rid it of the impurities which made up about twenty per cent of the weight of the linen cloth when it was taken off the loom. The cloth had to be boiled in a solution of potash which could be made by burning various substances including sea-weed.[1] Even in the mid-eighteenth century each piece of cloth had to be boiled perhaps as many as seven times and after each boiling it was spread out on the bleachgreen and watered. This operation required a full summer and the bleachers tried to shorten the process. In 1756 dilute sulphuric acid replaced a solution made from fermented bran and this change enabled the bleachers to complete three bleaches in the year instead of two.

The great revolution in bleaching which enabled the bleachers to bleach all the year round did not take place until the end of the century. Until then the linen-drapers bought most of their cloth in the first half of the year. Therefore the weavers had to work especially hard in the first half of the year knowing that after the month of June there would be far fewer opportunities for them to sell their webs at a reasonable profit. During the remainder of the summer they worked in the bleach-greens or cutting fuel in the turf-bogs or on their own small-holdings. Then they worked at the harvests of oats, wheat and finally potatoes before getting back to the loom to weave for the markets in the new year.

Since the weaver worked in his own home his time was his own. After market-day he might take things easily for a day or two and then work intermittently for the next few days. When the pressure was on him to finish a web for the next market he was quite prepared to sit up

1. Indeed many people on the sea-shore made a living by burning kelp and the rents on Rathlin Island, off the north coast, were paid from the proceeds.

The Great COCK MAIN,

BETWEEN the Gentlemen of Dromore and thofe of Banbridge and Donochclony, will be fought at the Cock-pit of Dromore upon Tuefday, Wednefday, Thurfday and Friday the 21ft, 22d, 23d, and 24th days of April inftant. It will confift of 31 battles, for four guineas each, and forty guineas the main or odd battle.

There will alfo be fought at faid place between faid parties, a Stag-Main of the fame number of battles, for the like fums, to begin the third Tuefday of June next. Dated this 7th of April, 1761.

N. B. The Cocks and Stags will be fhewed and weighed the Monday before the firft day of their refpective fightings.

all night before the market. The incentive to finish a web was often intensified by the need to buy provisions. If the cost of provisions was low and the price of linens high there wasn't the same need to finish the web and less cloth was brought to market. When the cost of provisions was high then the weaver had to work harder to feed his family and the linen-drapers knew that there would be more cloth in the market. It was no wonder that Arthur Young heard the drapers say in Lurgan in 1776 that they wished the price of oatmeal would never fall below one penny per pound: when it did the poor spent too much of their time in whiskey-houses. In fact this well-known phenomenon in the trade found expression in the proverb: 'A dear peck [= 9 lbs] of meal makes a cheap pack of yarn.'

Work at the loom was monotonous and many a weaver was glad of the excuse to leave his loom for a spree if the work was not too pressing. In north Armagh Arthur Young found them 'keeping packs of hounds, every man one, and joining; they hunt hares: a pack of hounds is never heard but all the weavers leave their looms and away they go after them by hundreds.' The blood-sport of cock-fighting was a traditional favourite with them and many weavers bred cocks for the ring and would walk miles to make a match and a wager. They loved horse-race meetings of which the most important was the Maze, near Lisburn, and Commodore Watson of Brookhill once remarked that he knew a ragged weaver to bet as much as twenty guineas on the result of a race there.

The weavers had the reputation of being 'licentious and disorderly'. There is no doubt that they were seriously involved in the Oakboy troubles of the 1760s and the Steelboy disturbances of the 1770s, both

Advertisement for cock-fighting in Dromore, county Down. Stags in this case were not male deer but young cocks not a year old (*Belfast Newsletter* 10 April 1761).

of which were directed against the burdens placed on them by the construction of new roads. The weavers were certainly the main protagonists in the fighting which broke out in County Armagh in the years after 1785 and culminated in the sectarian pitched battles of the mid-1790s between the Protestant Peep o' Day Boys and the Roman Catholic Defenders.

ARTICLES for Races to be run on the Courfe of Rich-hill, on Tuefday, Wednefday, Thurfday, Friday and Saturday, the 7th, 8th, 9th, 10th and 11th of July next, viz.

I. On Tuefday the 7th. A Purfe of twenty pounds will be run for by four year-olds, carrying nine ftone, faddle and bridle included, the beft of three three mile heats.—II. On Wednefday the 8th. A Purfe of ten pounds will be run for by real hunters, which can be proved to be fuch the laft feafon, carrying twelve ftone, faddle and bridle included, the beft of three four-mile heats.—III. On Thurfday the 9th. A Purfe of twenty pounds will be run for by any horfe, mare or gelding that never won at any one time above forty pounds carrying ten ftone, faddle and bridle included, the beft of three four-mile heats.—IV. On Friday the 10th. A Purfe of fifteen pounds will be run for by five-year-olds, fix year-olds, and aged horfes, mares, or geldings; five year olds carrying nine ftone two pounds, the fix year-olds carrying ten ftone, and the aged carrying ten ftone eight pounds, faddle and bridle included, the beft of three four-mile heats.—V. On Saturday the 11th, A large Purfe will be run for by the beaten cattle, carrying nine ftone, faddle and bridle included, the beft of three four-mile heats.

Any horfe; &c. winning two heats to be intitled to the prize. No croffing or jostling to be allow'd. Every horfe, &c. that ftarts for any of the above prizes to pay one fhilling in the pound entrance; and the winning horfe, &c. one fhilling in the pound for fcales and ftraw: Horfes, &c. to be enter'd with Henry Hutchefon of Richhill, clerk of the courfe, fix days before the refpective days of running, and kept in town at the houfe of a publican, who is a fubfcriber as fuch, or pay double entrance at the poft. No fcrub to be admitted to qualify. No lefs than two to ftart for any of the above prizes. Any horfe, &c. that wins any one prize is not intitled to ftart for any other: Half an hour allow'd for rubbing: All difputes to be determined by judges that will be appointed each day. The time of ftarting to be at three of the clock each day. No tent or booth to be erected on or near faid courfe but by a fubfcriber, as a publican, or other kind of goods fold but by the approbation of the clerk of the courfe

N. B. There will be a Stag Main every forenoon each day.

Advertisement for horse-racing at Richhill in County Armagh (*Belfast Newsletter* 16 June 1761)

35

The
KING and Constitution.
Loyal Orange
G. R.
Association
of the City of ARMAGH.
No. 509

We, the Master, Deputy-Master, and Secretary of the *LOYAL ORANGE ASSOCIATION*, Number 109 held in *Armagh in the county of Armagh* do hereby certify, that Brother *John Guilford* has regularly received the *............* Degree of a TRUE ORANGE-MAN, in this our Association; and that he has conducted himself, during his stay amongst us, to the entire satisfaction of all our Brethren.—We therefore request, that all the regular Associations of the Universe do recognize and admit him as such.

Given under our Hands and Seal of our Society, at *Armagh* — this *6th* Day of *July 1803*

Thomas Jackson Master.
Benjamin Jenkinson Deputy-Master.
Wm Clewlow Secretary.

Orange certificate (Armagh Museum 13—62).

The relationship between Catholics and Protestants had certainly been affected throughout the eighteenth century by the great expansion of the linen industry. The changes were explained in 1795 by Robert Stephenson, probably the most knowledgeable expert on the linen industry in the eighteenth century:

It is not to be expected that the manufacture could increase in so great a degree since 1771 as every description of the inhabitants were then fully employed in the progression of it, so that an increase must depend on an influx or increase of population. And it is to be observed that the Roman Catholics scarcely ever became weavers until after the year 1740. They considered it as a manufacture introduced by the Protestants or Huguenots tending to change their religion, and they preferred for many years being labourers to that of being weavers. However that prejudice is now totally worn out in Ulster, and there are good linenweavers of all professions [religions] . But it is worth notice that few if any Roman Catholics are head bleachers in the North, and still more extraordinary on looking into this great manufacture in Ulster which employed at least three millions sterling to carry it on, that it is almost every shilling in the hands of Protestants, as it is believed there are not four bleachyards in the hands of Roman Catholics, and those of little consequence when compared with the extensive works in their neighbourhood. Strange as this may appear it will bear examination.

PRONI D. 562/1270 (see page 76).

It must have been difficult for Catholic linen-drapers to break into the trade because the prejudice against them was reinforced by their lack of experience and knowledge of the trade. The increasing demand from England for cloth, however, broke down this barrier because the orders could not be fulfilled without a great expansion of the number of people engaged in the industry.

We have no knowledge of united-action being taken by linen-weavers to improve their rates of pay except the Lisburn riots of 1762 against new laws enforcing the inspection of brown linen in the markets. They paraded through the town carrying blackthorn sticks, attacked the drapers who did not agree with their views, and were finally dispersed by the military when pillaging a draper's house.

Generally, however, the interests of government and the linen-weavers did not clash and their societies appear to have been mainly ceremonial in character. A report from the *Belfast News-Letter*, dated 20 April 1753, noted that

. . . on Monday the 16th instant being the memorable day the Duke of Cumberland gained a complete victory over the rebel army in Scotland at Culloden Moore, William Brownlow Esquire [who was then seeking nomination for the County Armagh seat in the Irish Parliament] gave a most elegant entertainment at his house. And after dinner between two and three hundred of the linen weavers of Lurgan, all decently dressed with blue cockades in honour of the day, assembled themselves in the court before his house with music, drums, and the colours belonging to their society, where, after drinking His Majesty, the Duke of Cumberland and many other loyal toasts, with that of the day, they marched in regular order to town with the gentlemen freeholders at their head, drew up in order in the street and repeated the same loyal toasts they drank, also many particularly relative the Protestant interest, the linen manufacture, and the County of Armagh, and thence they returned to Mr. Brownlow's house and concluded the night with all demonstrations of joy.

The *Belfast News-Letter* referred on two occasions, in 1756 and 1765, to similar parades by the weavers in Belfast with drums, colours, and music.

Throughout the eighteenth century, indeed, the skilled weaver was an important and respected figure in Ulster. In a vigorous society he was looked on as a good tradesman who, with his family, could earn a regular and considerable income. His independence was reflected in his attitudes to authority and so Ulster politics became more democratic and the Protestant Churches more fragmented. The decline in his fortunes and in those of the cottier-weavers during the nineteenth century was to have a serious effect on the life of the Ulster community.

The Development of the Putting-out System

In the *Belfast News-Letter* of 25 March 1763 the following advertisement appeared:

Whereas John Corner weaver on the 18th day of March did absent himself from the town of Lurgan and took or sold in said town of Lisburn sundries yarn he had from several manufacturers to weave in and about said town; now in order to discountenance the like practices and to bring said Corner to the punishment the law has made and provided in these cases, we whose names are hereunto subscribed do promise a reward of three guineas . . . .

Said John Corner is fifty-five years old, about five feet nine inches, well-made, has a great stoop, very round-shouldered, and is remarkable for taking a large pinch of snuff; wore when he went off a large ash-coloured white coat and velvet cape not his property, a brown thick-set coat and buckskin breeches.

[Signed] Archibald Shaw, William Boyes, Thomas Bowen.

Water colour sketch of a linen-draper's premises in Lurgan built in the early nineteenth century (PRONI D.1464/2)

John Corner had taken yarn from each of these 'manufacturers', or merchants, to weave on the understanding that whenever a web was finished he would bring it to the merchant who would pay John Corner for weaving it. This system is known simply as 'putting out' because the manufacturer was putting out the work to be done by the weaver. Corner knew that when he brought the finished cloth to the merchant, he would not be so well paid as a weaver who had made the cloth from his own yarn. At the same time, however, he was being guaranteed the sale of his web at a price agreed between himself and the merchant. It is likely that he could not afford to buy the yarn direct from the yarn dealers in the market because it was well known that the weavers valued their independence so highly that they would take yarn from the merchants only when they could not buy it for themselves.

As the industry grew there was less chance of weavers being able to grow the bulk of the flax they needed and so more of them needed to buy in the markets. Whenever they could not afford to lay out the money to purchase yarn they had to take it on credit. Then they could easily fall into the situation described by Lord Abercorn's agent in 1759 when reporting about yarn-spinners who could not pay their rents:

James Hamilton, (5 July, 1759) PRONI (Abercorn Letters) T.2541/IA1/5/102.

The people that are backward [in paying] were, as I understand, much in debt as well for their rents and tithes as for their subsistence in our late hard times; to discharge which they got money advanced, mostly by yarn buyers to whom they are obliged to give their yarn as they spun it at such an undervalue; nor durst they dispute any price offered them by the lenders as that would destroy their credit with them . . . .

When times were bad the weaver who had no other resources found it hard to make a living and was ready to sacrifice his independence by taking work from a merchant to keep his family and himself alive. In these circumstances the putting-out trade could develop.

Yet as soon as good times returned both the spinner and weaver were able to free themselves from the putting-out system. Prices for their work rose and if the merchant were not prepared to pay high enough prices they could sell in the open markets. Then the merchant would complain that his agreements with the spinners and weavers were being broken, but there was little he could do. After all he needed to keep on good terms with the spinners and weavers. Putting-out could only establish itself completely when the merchant controlled the supply of raw materials.

It was the cotton industry which really introduced the putting-out system on an extensive scale into the north of Ireland in the 1780s. The cotton-weavers attended at the merchant's warehouse to obtain the quantity of yarn they required and brought back the finished web. The merchant was, therefore, able to state the terms on which he would give out the yarn. Some of the cotton-weavers did at first try to weave on their own account but found that they could not sell their webs in bad times and so they went back to the security of the putting-out system.

The cotton industry established itself in the north and east of Ireland very easily because it paid higher wages to the weavers. Indeed the wages were so high and the prospects so attractive that many weavers moved into Belfast to be near the spinning mills.

The earnings of a good weaver of muslin with constant employment, that is, when not kept waiting for his yarn either to put in or to carry on his web, is from eighteen shillings to a guinea per week, more than double the wages of a linen weaver: some time ago it was more; and when to this is added the price of winding the yarn [paid by the manufacturer], it must be allowed that the introduction of a muslin loom into a family must be an object of considerable importance. Indeed the change of dress and deportment in this class of persons was very obvious to everyone, and a smart young cotton weaver became no slight attraction in the eyes of a country belle.

Dubourdieu, *Statistical Survey ... C*
Down (1802), pp.236–7.

The writer admitted in this passage written in 1802 that 'some time ago it [the money which a cotton-weaver could earn] was more'. The accompanying table shows just how rapidly piece rates (the price paid by the manufacturer to the weaver for weaving each piece of cloth) did fall in the Belfast cotton weaving industry between 1792 and 1838. This was caused mainly by the increasing use throughout the British Isles of the power-loom to weave cotton. Wages were pushed lower and lower as the weavers tried to hold their own against competition from machinery. Some idea of the hardships they must have suffered can be seen from a study of the following table.

TABLE SHOWING THE DECLINE IN THE WEEKLY EARNINGS OF COTTON WEAVERS AND WHAT IT MEANT TO THEIR STANDARD OF LIVING.

	Weaver's weekly av. earnings	Potatoes per cwt.	Oatmeal per cwt.	Annual rent of 4-loom house
1792-99	£2.33	—	—	£5.83
1799-1806	£1.92	£0.14	£0.93	£6.83
1806-13	£1.58			£6.83
1813-20	£1.08	£0.13	£0.92	£6.83
1820-27	£0.63	£0.12	£0.66	£5.50
1827-34	£0.33	£0.08	£0.63	£5.00
1834-38	£0.31	£0.09	£0.57	£5.00

Whereas in the 1780s cotton cloth had been a luxury it became the cheapest and commonest material for clothing by the 1820s. This seriously affected the linen industry which had to compete with cotton, and forced many manufacturers to bring in more efficient techniques and methods of organisation. The bleachers who saw what was happening to the trade cut their costs of production by introducing chlorine for bleaching: this greatly reduced the time required for bleaching. In fact bleaching, which had been previously confined to the summer months, became an all-the-year-round operation, for the ancient belief

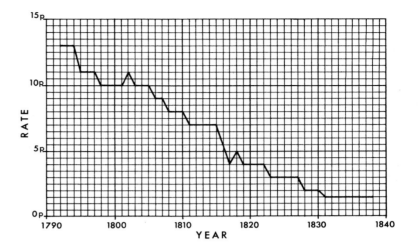

RATE

YEAR

The decline in the piece work rates of a Belfast cotton handloom weaver from 1792-1838 for weaving a piece of jaconet.

died that frost damaged linens bleaching on the grass. The weavers, too, in an effort to keep up their average earnings in a period when life was getting harder for them, began to adopt the *flying shuttle* for their looms. It speeded up weaving so much that the time to finish a web was halved. Although the flying shuttle had been invented seventy years earlier (1733) for the weaving of wool, it was not introduced into Ireland until about 1776 and was taken up first by the cotton-weavers.

The women who spun the linen yarn, however, were to suffer first and most severely. Their earnings fell suddenly and it became impossible to make a living from spinning. There was no need for a linen-yarn merchant to go to the expense of building a factory, installing machinery, and employing people to work it as long as he could buy hand-spun yarn so cheaply. An Ulster manufacturer explained the situation in 1811:

The leading cause against the extension of machinery is the low price of labour; yarn spun by women is sold here much cheaper than the same article manufactured by machinery in England. In the latter country, the labouring classes have a choice of employments in consequence of the variety of its manufacturers. If one fail them, they can apply to another: with us the case is different. When the trade is bad its worst effects are felt by the poor women, who must sell at the prices of the day or remain unemployed, and it frequently happens that they dispose of the worked article for less than the raw material cost them. To one unacquainted with Ireland, the small earnings of the poorer females — frequently not more than two-pence per day working diligently from morning till night for months together — must appear very extraordinary; and under such circumstances it is unlikely that this trade should increase so much as it might, though spurred on in the beginning by offers of large premiums from the Linen Board.

With the aid of machinery, one person is fully equal to do the work of ten, and in this the advantage in its favour appears to be great; yet

E. Wakefield, *An account of Ireland, statistical and political* (London, 1812), I, p.684.

when it is considered that women are fully competent to bring any description of yarn which we spin to double the fineness that machinery can, this advantage is much lessened.

Another thing against us is that we cannot with any material, let its quality be what it may, exceed the fineness of three hanks or thirty-six leas in the pound, whereas women when the flax is good can run it from twelve to twenty hanks, or from 144 to 240 leas in the pound.

Our yarn, from the better quality of the raw material, is superior. It sells, therefore, considerably higher, and is commonly used as warp for yarn spun by hand.

On balancing the account we believe the advantages are in favour of mill-spinning; and we are of opinion that this improvement will, one time or other, become a source of prosperity to the country.

The wages in the factories may on an average be eight pence per day, and spinners could not be procured for much less; in their own houses they are satisfied with fourpence or fivepence.

To sum up the whole, the quantity of yarn spun by machinery, the greater price given for it, and the better means of obtaining a market, are in favour of that mode with respect to coarse yarn. On the other hand, the low price of labour, the superior fineness of the wrought material, and the expense of machinery with its wear and tear, are very great drawbacks; yet it may be estimated that the balance is in favour of the former to the amount, it is supposed, of one halfpenny per hank, or twelve leas.

'Flowering' linen i.e. embroidering flower patterns on linen, in County Down (Welch Collection, Ulster Museum).

LONDONDERRY.

Firms in the city of Londonderry engaged in shirt-making in 1909 listed in *Macdonald's Irish Directory and Gazetteer* of that year.

In the opinion of this manufacturer, therefore, the balance in 1811 was slightly in favour of mill-spun yarn. Some of the Ulster manufacturers began to import English mill-spun yarn and it was estimated, for example, that John Cromie of Diaper Hill, near Castlewellan, put out work to between 2,000 and 3,000 weavers. These manufacturers boiled, sorted, and prepared all the yarn on their own premises and gave it out to women to wind into the hanks for the weavers.

The balance between hand-spun and mill-spun yarn swung decisively in favour of mill-spun yarn when James Kay of Preston in 1825 patented the wet-spinning process by which fine yarns could be spun in the mills. Within ten years ten big mills had been built in Ulster to use the new process and by 1838 there were sixty-four throughout Ireland. The domestic spinning industry was ruined in eastern Ulster. The loss of income from spinning was serious throughout Ulster for only in some areas were women able to get other employment. Some of them wound yarn for the manufacturers while others worked at home sewing muslin or doing white embroidery known as sprigging. The Derry shirt making industry also began in this period employing women who used to spin and by the second half of the nineteenth century it put out shirts to be sewn in places over thirty miles from Derry.

The fact that Ulster manufacturers had built ten mills so soon after the invention of the wet-spinning process in 1825, showed that they were worried about the success of their competitors in Scotland and Yorkshire. The mill owners in Scotland and Yorkshire had concentrated so successfully on the spinning of coarse yarns that the Irish manufacturers not only could not sell their cloth in England but were losing their Irish markets. The handloom weavers of Drogheda suffered very severely while the weavers of the western counties such as Donegal, Sligo, and Mayo were driven out of the industry. In County Sligo where, about 1820, 400-500 webs had been sold in Sligo town and 100-150 in Collooney every week, scarcely any cloth was brought to the market in 1838. In that year a government official reported on the collapse of the industry there and the consequences he feared:

Mills for the spinning of yarn have not been established, and the expense on the transit of mill-spun yarn has prevented linen manufacturers from giving out webs to weavers to be made up. The consequence has been, that the linen manufacture on the old system has died a natural death, and the new system not being introduced in its stead, linen weaving, except for farmers' use, has become extinct . . . .

The state of the linen trade in those districts of the west and south of Ireland where it had been established is not in general dissimilar from the state of the trade in the county of Sligo, and has been affected by similar causes. Linen weaving is chiefly confined to the making up webs for the use of the peasantry, except in a few districts where the almost total absence of any employment for the great mass of the people has rendered hand-loom labour so cheap as to enable some webs of coarse cloth to be occasionally made up on the old system, so cheap as to afford a profit to the few jobbers who continue to frequent the linen markets . . . . The quality of linens offered for sale is daily deteriorating, the looms of the weavers are in a bad state of repair and of the worst

construction, and in some districts (Dingle in the County Kerry, for instance) the weavers use the hand in place of the fly shuttle.

    . . . . Even now the webs brought in for sale to the brown [linen] markets of Mayo and Kerry would scarcely find purchasers, were it not for the remoteness of these districts from the principal towns of Ireland, their want of intercourse with the capital, and the difficulty and delays of procuring goods from thence, owing to the imperfect means of carriage.

It is clear that if the linen industry in Ireland had not been reorganised by the men who built the big spinning mills it would have been destroyed by the more efficient English and Scottish firms who were able to sell their cloth at much lower prices than had been usual in the eighteenth century. These men often came from families which had made money in the linen trade in the eighteenth century and were ready to invest it in large undertakings to secure the future of the industry.

The linen manufacturers in the neighbourhood of Banbridge not only give out linen webs to weavers on an extensive scale, but have also established numerous mills for the spinning of yarn, and extensive bleach greens. Many of the manufacturers spin their own yarn and bleach their own cloth, and all of them either dispose of their goods at their own offices to the agent of their customers, export them directly from Belfast, or consign them there to the great linen factors who dispose of them on commission.

The success of the cotton mill owners and then of the Yorkshire and Scottish linen mill owners had shown the Irish manufacturer the advan-

James Murland's spinning mill at Annsborough, near Castlewellan, County Down: the first wet spinning mill in Ulster. *(HMSO)*

Reports of assistant commissioners on handloom weavers (1840).

Entry for James Murland's spinning mill in the First Valuation field book, 1838 (PRONI VAL 1B/380).

Houses in Townland of Ballylough

No.	Name and Description.	Quality Letter.	Length.	Breadth.	Height.	Number of Measures.	Rate per Measure.	Amount. £	s.	d.
	~~Saml Shaw~~									
6 9	James Murland ~~Esq~~									
	Office, Store & hackling shop	1A	49.0 av	25.6	21.0	124.9	12 3/4	6	12	11 1/4 ~~8~~
	Office, Bundling shed	1A	88.0	13.0	6.6	114.4	5	2	7	8
	Office (factory) 31.6 high	1A	87.0	40.0	33.0	348.0	17 1/4	25	0	3
1/8 off	Office, Boilor house	1A	13.0	21.0	20.6	27.3	12 1/2	1	8	4 1/2
	Office (Engine house)	1A	32.0	14.0	22.6 av	44.8	13 1/4	2	9	10 1/2
1/4 off	Office Boiler house for steam Engine	1A	55.0	13.6	22.6	74.2	13 1/4	4	1	10 1/2
1/6 off	Office (Gas house)	1A	20.0	24.0	11.0	48.0	7 1/2	1	10	0
1/3 off	Office, Shed	1A	20.6	8.6	6.6	17.4	5	0	7	3
1/20 off	Office (forge)	1A	23.6	21.6	7.6	50.5	5 1/2	1	3	1 1/2
								45	0	11 1/4

Diameter of water wheel 21.6 – 8 feet wide
water fall 16.6 – depth of shrouding 2 feet – Metal wheel
2634 Spindles for spinning fine yarn — 1/8 0 3 6 1/4; 1/4 1 0 5 1/2; 1/6 0 5 0; 1/3 0 2 5; 1/20 0 1 1 3/4
with Cards & hackling for same, & preparing — 1 12 6 1/2
£130 There are 1360. 1 3/4 Inch Small Spindles — Amount 43 8 4 3/4
and 1250. 2 Inch (large ones) & 24. 4 Inch – for twine — 31 10 0
letter of machinery A 10 1/2 months work ~~water~~ power — ~~50~~
12 hours a day – they have only apply'd — ~~£95 8 4~~
the Steam power 12 days this Summer, which — 74 18 4
was 1/2 the power during the time employed – 1/3 — 24 19 8
and the Superintendent Supposes that the — £49 19 0
Steam power applied each year amounts to
about 6 weeks work of the entire power
by taking the average since he came, now 3 years

tages of putting out work to the weavers. No longer did the bleacher or his agents need to tour the brown linen markets buying cloth. He was able to pay the manufacturer well if he could promptly supply any quantity of the kinds of linen he required to meet his order. The manufacturer's reputation was a guarantee of quality so he ensured that the weavers produced cloth to an acceptable standard. Since there were so many weavers throughout the countryside the manufacturer was able to make them compete to work for him. He could refuse work to anyone who did not satisfy him and he could fine weavers out of their earnings for not completing their webs on time or for faults in their cloth. The extent of the manufacturer's authority is shown by the conditions laid down on a typical weaver's ticket.

		lbs	oz
No.	24 Hd.	5	8
Breadth 34½ In.	65 Weft	4	8

No wages promised. Weaving paid according to the manner the work is executed. Four weeks allowed for working; if more, 2d. per day will be taken off the wages. Tallow must not be used in dressing; and if candle grease, or oil from spindle, be on the linen, there will be a heavy fine.

August 21, 1838.   *J. Murland*

The disappearance of the independent handloom weavers and the brown linen markets did not occur suddenly. The handloom weavers valued their traditional independence. As one weaver expressed it: 'The reason I did not turn to work for manufacturers was, I had a sort of pride in me, and having a little farm I did not wish to be subject to fines if I had not my web in by a certain time.' In saying this he spoke for many of the weavers of fine linen in the Lurgan-Tanderagee area of County Armagh. To accept work from a manufacturer was felt by such men to be something of a disgrace and so throughout Ulster many of those who had small farms gave up weaving altogether. They would not accept terms as were laid down by this Lisburn manufacturer:

I agree that I will weave all yarns which I take from the office of James N Richardson, Sons & Co., into good and sufficient cloth, in — weeks at the farthest from date of delivery of the same; and that all cloth wove by me shall be left for inspection at the office, without appealing from whatever decision may be passed there.

          [Witness]   [Signature]
     [Date]

Most of the weavers soon found, however, that the earnings of those employed by the manufacturers were higher than their own. The manufacturers could also provide more regular work for their employees and such security was especially valuable to a weaver who had a home and family to keep, whenever yarn was scarce or dear in the market. In hard times such weavers were tempted to take work from the manufacturer. They soon found, too, that it was convenient to have everything prepared for them by the manufacturer. The preparation of yarn

Child's ticket issued by Londonderry shipping agent for transatlantic passage to Philadelphia in the United States of America in 1844 (PRONI T.2511/2).

for the loom had always been an expensive and time-consuming chore whereas the mill-spun yarn was ready to put on the loom. The weaver was pleased to find mill-spun yarn much easier and quicker to weave for he had often complained that the poor quality of homespun, which was now all that he could buy, caused frequent breaks. When he had finished the web he knew what he would be paid for it whereas the independent weaver wasted much of his time hawking the cloth through the markets fearing that in the end he might have to sell it at a loss. The buyer would say that the price should be lower because there was no demand for linen or because there was too much brought to market; yarn might be too dear or labour too plentiful. In every case it was the independent weaver who suffered and so it is not surprising that within fifteen years

Letter written from Quebec in 1832 by John and Eliza Anderson, emigrants from Londonderry (PRONI D.1859/1).

with the ice I saw more ice on the banks of new
foundland or rather the northren Coasts nor if
I had lived in ireland to the age of methuselam
and for size we had it from the smallest piece to
the largeist hill in knockaduff you may think
our state was miserable when the Captain was seen
droping teers the Captain and mate went up to
the masthead and found us inclosed in every side
but we had redson to bless god for his mercys unto
us the sea was very Calm we had as good a
Captain as ever sailed the sea he was never seen
intoxicated the symmetry is a fine brig only she
sprung a lake and had to be pumped day and
night from the 6th of May untill we landed
in Quebec we had little sickness on sea Eliza
was eight days sea sick Mary and Jane had there

49

health. pritty well on sea and as for me I have reason to bless god for his mercys I never had an hours sickness since I left Ballinree and that is a grate blessing it has pleased the lord to visit Quebec with the Colera of Morbus and it is rageing here to ≠ a grate extent it has carried of upwards of three thousand people it has pleased the lord to visit our little famely by a stroke of death little Jane is no more she took bad on the 13th of June and died the 17 we had the docter with her he did not think she died with the Colera of Morbus he thought it was drop on the brain she was buried about four oclock in evening and she was fiftieth corps entred the graveyard that day and 28 of them lying unburied you need not write to me untill I send you another letter I'ad not but remains your son and Daughter John & Eliza Anderson

of the introduction of the process of spinning fine yarns by machinery, the majority of Ulster weavers were employed by manufacturers.

Some of the independent weavers gave up weaving altogether and began to concentrate on their small farms. Many of them found they could make more money by growing flax for the mills. The improvement in the quality of farming was soon noticed by people travelling through the north-eastern counties for the weavers had been notorious for their bad farming. Other weavers emigrated to Canada and the United States and even to Scotland. It has even been said that the fall in the standard of living caused by the changes of the linen industry was the most important factor in encouraging emigration from County Londonderry at this time.

It was generally recognised that those weavers who remained in the trade were a poorer class than the independent weavers of the previous century. As early as 1821 it was remarked about the Raphoe area in County Donegal

that twenty years ago there was scarcely a common weaver who had not ten pounds to lend whereas an equal sum would at this day purchase almost any individual of that class out of a habitation [i.e. it would buy his house]. It was usual at that time for the farming heads of families to put their younger sons into this employment, many of whom were enabled by proper economy and application in a few years to purchase farms, but this practice has been long discontinued.

In the Rathfriland area of County Down it was noted in 1840:

The farmers were formerly the manufacturing weavers and divided their attention between the loom and their farm. The class who now work for employers formerly composed those who worked occasionally as day labourers for hire for the farmers, either on their land or on their looms.

The weavers soon realised, however, that the 'good old times' had vanished in the linen industry. An impartial expert found that the average weekly earnings of a linen-weaver in Ireland on one loom about 1840 ranged from three shillings to about eight shillings. Whenever the foreign demand for linen fell there was a 'slack time' and workers were laid off. Wages had to be cut by the employers whenever flax was scarce and dear. The weavers could not protect their interests because there were too many of them needing work. The introduction of mill-spun yarn enabled women and boys to weave and they soon became the majority of all weavers. Apprenticeships were of no further value in the eyes of the manufacturers who relied on the system of fining the weavers for poor workmanship. The handloom weaver had slipped from his high position in the scale of trades until he became the poorest. As one man put it' 'I think if the agricultural labourers could get constant employment here they would be better off than the handloom weavers.'

Every manufacturer knew from experience the disadvantages of putting yarn out for the weavers to weave in their own time in comparison with the more efficient system of working in factories. Even if the manufacturer did fine his weavers every time their cloth was de-

51

livered late or contained flaws, he would never manage to make them as disciplined and efficient a work force as those who wove under his personal supervision in the factory. He might give them bonuses for good work but they were so used to working at their own pace that they rarely heeded incentives; weaving was such a monotonous job that a self-employed weaver would seize any opportunity to leave his loom to see or take part in anything exciting. So often was the weaver late in finishing his web that one employer remarked that he would not take an order that he would be obliged to give to his outweavers to make up, for if he was obliged to give them an order for a thousand pieces he would have to give out one thousand five hundred in order to get the thousand done in time.

When the weaver brought back his completed web to the manufacturer's office, the cloth had to be checked very thoroughly to see that it had been properly woven and that enough threads had been used to weave it. In many cases the webs were deficient because weavers or their families were often tempted, either by greed or circumstances, to sell some of the yarn they had been given.

Counterfoiled note detailing the terms of the contract according to which cloth was to be woven from the yarn given out by the manufacturer (PRONI D.1113).

Some manufacturers would give out yarn only to those weavers who could get substantial householders to act as their securities (PRONI D.2057).

52

(ORIGINAL.)

PETTY SESSIONS (IRELAND) ACT, 1851, 14 & 15 VICT., CAP. 93.

(FORM B a.) SUMMONS.

James Johnston
Linen Manufacturer
Complainant ; Petty Sessions District of *Crumlin.*

William Moore
Crew
Defendant. County of Antrim.

(1) CAUSE OF COMPLAINT, with Time and Place.

WHEREAS a complaint has been made to me that (1) you have detained a quantity of Linen Yarn which was entrusted to you to weave into Linen Cloth, it being the Complainant's property

To
The Defendant

This is to command you to appear as a Defendant on the Hearing of said Complaint, at the COURT-HOUSE, CRUMLIN, on MONDAY, the *16th* day of *July* 18*60* at Eleven o'clock, in the forenoon, before such Justices as shall be there.

Signed,

this *6th* *July* 18*60*

Justice of said County.

Crumlin (County Antrim) petty sessions summons against a weaver by a linen manufacturer for not returning the cloth he had undertaken to weave (PRONI D.766/14).

On the old system, when the weavers used to weave on their own account, the selling or pawning of weft was always the readiest means of supplying the present necessities of the needy, or the means to which the members of a weaver's family resorted to procure a supply of tea, tobacco, or whiskey. Thus a vast number of hucksters' shops were called into existence in the weaving districts, and these discounted the drafts of weft in the debased and debasing currency of stimulants [= alcohol]. Cops of weft were in many cases the weavers' currency and the accomodating dealer asked no questions, for conscience sake.

On the change of weavers working on the property of others instead of their own, the difference was not always remembered; old habits

53

were not to be overcome by nice distinctions; the tempting doors of the accomodating and unscrupulous huckster are still open for the weft; a few cops are not missed; and besides, there is the intention of replacing them before the work is finished.

Quite a lot of fuss was made about weavers embezzling yarn but it was not so serious as it sounded, for comparatively small quantities could have been involved and inspection of the webs was a sufficiently effective deterrent. What probably did worry a manufacturer, if he stopped to think about it, was that his property was in the hands of very poor people to weave and the only control that he had over them was their need for payment. It must have been a sobering thought.

In effect the manufacturer was dependent to a considerable extent on the loyalty of his outworkers. This did place a burden of responsibility on the shoulders of some manufacturers but whenever they saw the price of cloth falling steadily in foreign markets they realised their own survival in business would depend on cutting the scale of payments to the outweavers. So the payment for weaving a piece of fine cambric fell from sixty shillings to forty shillings between 1828 and 1852 and that for weaving coarser cambric was cut by nearly half from seventeen shillings to eight shillings and sixpence.

As long as the outweavers were prepared to accept such severe cuts in their earnings, manufacturers could afford to give them work. But the Great Famine checked this trend. So many people died in Ireland and so many emigrated from it that there was a severe shortage of all kinds of workers and so the earnings of the outweavers rose smartly — by between twenty and thirty per cent, over five years. One manufacturer of the period described the result:

So long as a man's labour could be had at the handloom in Ireland for a shilling a day, it was felt no power loom could work much, if at all, cheaper; but when wages, some few years back, began to increase and the population to decrease instead of increase, it was admitted that the power loom was at length required.

W. Charley, *Flax and its products in Ireland* (London, 1862) p.88.

Indeed, the piece-rates for handloom weaving fell so low that in the 1840s English and Scots manufacturers sent over yarn to be woven in Ireland. A letter written by a County Londonderry landowner in the autumn of 1847 reveals that such employment had helped to save the people of one Ulster village from the worst effects of the Great Famine:

This district is particularly famous for its weavers, and strange to say, whilst the manufacturers are working short time or dismissing their people in Lancashire and Carlisle, the same men are sending over their yarn here to be woven in greater quantities than ever. There were two agents for English manufacturers in my village [Castledawson] last year. There are now five. The cause is evident: they get their work done as well here and at half the price. But what pleases me more than anything is that these competitors are bidding against each other for labour and they have actually doubled the price for weaving a web which they have hitherto given. This is the true principle of free trade, manufacturing in the cheapest market and not caring a damn for their own people, but certainly I shall not call out against them.

PRONI T.2603/3.

54

Women attending powerlooms in an Ulster weaving factory early in this century (Welch Collection, Ulster Museum).

After the Great Famine the number of power-looms began to increase rapidly as this table shows:

1857	1,691 power looms
1862	4,666
1867	14,834
1905	32,831

The number more than trebled in the five years between 1862 and 1867 when the linen industry had a great boom because the cotton manufacturers could not obtain American cotton during the American Civil War.

Yet the rise in the wages of the handloom outweavers was not great enough to compel every manufacturer to go to the expense of building a factory and purchasing power-looms. The initial cost of a factory and the continuous charges for the maintenance of the building and the machinery, required it to be in full production if it was to make a profit. In bad times it could become a huge white elephant eating up the firm's money. It is worth studying this description of a Lisburn factory written by its owner probably as an advertisement for its sale:

Particulars Lagan Factory

Lagan factory built on land situated on the banks of the Lagan in Lisburn 2 acres 2 roods 2 perches, held from Sir Richard Wallace at the yearly rent of £8.13s.6d. Lease is for 99 years from 1st May 1855 and same can be made for 10,000 years at the usual favourable terms of the estate.

The factory contains 101 looms, cost of which (including cost of lease and building) was £6,500. Extra to above and not counting ordinary repairs the looms were renewed in the late dull times in all their wearable parts at a cost of several hundreds. This was done to the satisfaction of the writer's foreman who informed him that the looms required no further outlay as they were then in first class order.

Suitable preparing for above including dressing machines, winding and warping machines. Sixteen horse [power] engine fitted to drive 300 looms with space in engine house for another engine. Two boilers having sufficient boiler space for engines working 300 looms.

Price List for 'Irish hand woven linen damask' cloths proposed to be exhibited at the Panama Pacific International Exposition in San Francisco, dated 1 February 1915 (PRONI D.1619/3).

Store and dwelling house. Yarn house with all advantages for steeping, etc., Abundance of water for engine, washing of yarn, etc.

Water carriage on coals from Belfast Quay to bank of Lagan at factory 2s.3d. per ton.

Factory was built with a view to extension and could be extended very cheaply.

The handloom weaving industry was seriously hit by the introduction of the power-loom and so it began to decline steadily. The handloom was still essential for weaving those fine threads which could not stand the strain of the power-loom but as improvements were continually being made to the power-loom it was clear that in the long run the power-loom would drive out the handloom for all but the finest work. Until the First World War broke out in 1914 the American market was prepared to pay for high quality damask linens especially for tablecloths and table napkins, and for fine cambrics which made excellent handkerchiefs. It was estimated, however, that in the ten years before 1907 the number of people engaged in the cambric industry had fallen by half, partly because the power mills had started to warp and wind the beams for the cambric looms, work which had previously been done by the weaver's family. Most of the damasks were woven in handloom workshops, known as factories (abbreviated form of manufactories: where items were made by hand), as they had been since the mid-eighteenth century; this was because they required careful supervision, while rigging a damask loom was a job for four or five men and therefore more convenient in workshops. The centre of this fine linens handloom industry was in the Lurgan-Waringstown-Portadown area.

Further north in the Ballymena area of County Antrim the domestic industry remained substantial until the end of the century. A lecturer in 1910 provided this picture of the industry in the second half of the nineteenth century.

Light shirting linens had their chief centre in Ballymena and a great amount of business was done there. In olden time, and until say fifty years ago the weaver himself brought his web into the market and sold

Patterns for handwoven damask cloths drawn between 1790–1820 for the firm of Coulson of Lisburn (PRONI D.1492/1)

it. By degrees that manner of doing business was superseded by a middleman or so-called manufacturer who bought yarn in large lots from the spinner, prepared the warps, and gave them out accompanied with sufficient weft, to the weaver. One of these manufacturers might succeed in having hundreds of weavers thus working for him. Forty years ago a hundred such manufacturers used to be present at the weekly Saturday market to dispose of the webs of linen which had been woven for them in the surrounding cottages.

Thirty years ago the webs offered for sale on a Saturday sometimes numbered 20,000. The York Street Flax Spinning Company have it on record that in 1880, in a timè of stagnation, the Ballymena manufacturers had a stock of 40,000 webs. These were worth about £3 per web, of which the weaver's wages had been something like £1 per web.

Ballymoney had a reputation for a rather better quality than Ballymena, and Coleraine a little better still. In County Down were woven the heaviest and best shirting linens. Armagh gave its name to the

Damask weaving. Notice that the temples are very close up to the reed on the cloth (Welch Collection, Ulster Museum).

R.WELCH. 1300X. LINEN HANDLOOM WEAVING.

Sir W. Crawford, *Irish linen and some features of its production* (1910), p.12.

Damask weaving. Notice the 'wing' hanging from the post on the first loom on the right. It was made from brown paper stretched and glued over a light wooden frame and was used by the weaver as a fan to dry the paste of flour and water with which the cloth was dressed on the loom (Welch Collection, Ulster Museum).

very coarse linens used as buckram and linings, the trade name of which was 'Armaghs'. Randalstown produced mosquito nettings and creole checks, which were largely shipped to New Orleans.

The handloom industry survived into the twentieth century but even as early as 1909 the British parliament had to pass the Handloom Weavers' Protection Act to revive the hand-weaving of damasks, cambrics, and diapers. It had no lasting success. Continuous improvements to modern looms and production methods rendered the handloom less and less capable of competing with the power-loom. Fewer young men took up handloom weaving since the wages did not compare with those of other trades. The craft of the handloom-weavers was taken to its grave by the old men.

AN ULSTER HANDLOOM WEAVING FACTORY.

The Weavers under the Putting-out System

Weaving is rather a popular trade in almost the whole of Ulster, for it is soon learned and requires little capital to buy the tools. The looms are generally hired, so much being paid annually for that purpose, so that the weaver when equipped with his shears, rubbing bone, and a few other similar articles, such as strings and thrums, is ready for his work. Like every other class of workmen, he has the characteristics peculiar to his craft. His labour is light, and as he performs his work sitting, using both arms and legs together, he exercises the whole body more or less, and obtains a very fair muscular development. He whiles away the tedious hours of the day by singing songs, of which he has generally a good stock, the posts of his loom are generally papered with the current ballad poetry of the day, and sometimes may be seen the portrait of some rustic or other beauty. He has always the new songs first in the country, for being oftener out in the market towns, and generally having a taste for such, he has his eye out for anything of the kind, and in this

Weaver's shears and rubbing stones (one of them is likely to have been a stone axehead). *(Armagh Museum)*

60

Harvest knot made from the heads of flax. *(Armagh Museum)*

way he becomes quite an authority amongst amazed and admiring rustics.

This portrait of the handloom weaver about 1860 could have been drawn by any casual visitor to the workshop. The writer was obviously not concerned with the everyday problems which the weaver had to face. Therefore his picture is shallow and superficial. He is not describing the same person that was portrayed in a letter written 23 February 1847 by a clergyman of the Church of England to the Relief Committee of the Society of Friends about the effects of the Great Famine in a parish in north Armagh:

The population of this parish has been hitherto chiefly supported by weaving, carried on in their own houses. The weaver at present can only earn, by weaving a web of sixty yards, two shillings and sixpence to four shillings and sixpence, which employs him nearly a whole week in preparation, while at present prices such wages will not support the mere weaver without a family.

Even with such wages, I can state it as a fact, having come under my own immediate observation, that weavers are sitting up three nights per week, in order by any means to procure food for their families. There is scarcely a family in the parish in which there is not one or more members of the family sitting up nightly. I have seen them on returning to my own home (from visiting the sick) at two a.m. working as busily as in the day time. In several cases I have relieved individuals in their own houses who from exhaustion had been compelled to lie down and could no longer continue to work at the loom.

This was the other side of the picture which haunted every handloom weaver during the hard times in his trade and finally drove many to leave it. The weaver was more tied to his loom than he had ever been. Sitting at a loom was not healthy work and the weaver's constitution was undermined by long hours and poor food. One writer went so far as to comment: 'I could not pass a weaver by without knowing him to be one; and I never saw a weaver that had not dyspepsia [indigestion] written in his countenance.'

The effect on the weaver and his family of the great changes which had taken place in the linen industry in the first half of the nineteenth century is well illustrated in this transcript of evidence given about 1840 to the Commission inquiring into the condition of the handloom weavers in the United Kingdom. The weaver was John Duff from County Armagh.

FORM 6.—REGISTRY of Persons Admitted into, and Discharged from the Workhouse

1. Number.	2. Names and Surnames of Paupers.	3. Sex.	4. Age.	5. If Adult, whether Single, Married, Widower, or Widow; if Child, whether Orphan, Deserted, or Bastard.	6. Employment or Calling.	7. Religious denomination.	8. If disabled, the description of disability.
9341 / 1731	Rogers Henry	Mc	74	Widower	Weaver	Quaker	Aged & Infirm
2	Telford George	Mc	22	Single	Weaver	Protestant	Healthy
3	Irwin Jane	F	63	Widow	Winder	Presbyterian	Aged & Infirm
4	Bogue Michael	Mc	30	Married	Labourer	RC Catholic	Healthy
5	" Mary	F	53	Wife of abov	Spinner	do	"
6	" John	Mc	13	Child of abov	None	do	do
7	" Mary	F	11	do	do	do	do
8	" Margaret	F	9	do	do	do	d
9	Wright Charlotte	F	25	Single	Labourer	RC Catholic	do
9330 / 1780	Bleaney Alice	F	8	Child of abov	None	"	do
1	Magilligan Anne	F	19	Single	Servant	RC Catholic	do
2	Pepper Samuel	Mc	60	Married	Blacksmith	Protestant	Aged & Infirm
3	" Samuel	Mc	12	Child of abov	None	do	Healthy
4	" Jane	F	10	do	do	do	do
5	" Mary	F	4	do	do	do	do
6	Blair Thomas	Mc	55	Married	Weaver	Presbyterian	do
7	" Betty	F	45	Wife of abov	Winder	do	do
8	" Margaret	F	13	Child of abov	None	do	do
9	" Wm	Mc	10	do	do	do	do
9340 / 1740	Brown Hannah	F	30	Widow	do	Protestant	do
1	Best John	Mc	11	Deserted	None	do	do
2	Watson E. Jane	F	13		do		do
3	Toale John	Mc	30	Single	Labourer	RC Catholic	Epileptic
4	Turkington John	Mc	54	Single	Weaver	Protestant	Healthy
5	Morrison Sarah	F	38	Married	Spinner	do	do
6	" Benjamin	Mc	5	Child of abov	None	do	do
7	Nicholson Grace	F	45	Single	Winder	do	do
8	Brown A. Jane	F	22	Single	Weaver	do	Delicate
9	Vass John	Mc	45	Married	Weaver	do	do
9350 / 1750	" Sarah	F	41	Wife of abov	Winder	do	do
1	" Margaret	F	15	Single. child of ab	do	do	do
2	" John	Mc	13	Child of 9349	do	do	do
3	" Elizabeth	F	11	do	None	do	do

I am a weaver and have been so for nearly forty years. The weavers generally are so poor that they cannot weave for the market as they formerly did but are compelled to take work from the manufacturers at whatever they can get. I remember when we had but two manufacturers in this part of the country and they paid good prices.

I think this increase of manufacturers has very much lessened the earnings of the poor; it has also produced a competition among them which reduced prices and with it wages; it has also deteriorated the quality of the goods. If a poor man has a shed or hovel to live in he must pay for it weekly, and to do so he must work at whatever prices he can get. The poverty of the people and their numbers always places it in the hands of the masters to pay what they please; a man can do nothing for himself.

A 12^{00} takes a man six or eight days to weave with a hand-shuttle but rather less with the fly-shuttle. The majority now use the fly-shuttle. About Laghore [Loughgall] they make from 3^{00} to 5^{00} and earn from 2s. downwards weekly; about 6d a set would be the average rate of weaving but rather more as you get to the higher numbers.

Great loss has been sustained by the weavers' families being thrown idle owing to the substitution of the mill yarn. Formerly a hand spinner would get 4½d. to 4d. a hank for spinning and now they have about 1½d. or 2d., at the outside, a hank where they [have] got it to do, but that is seldom the case now. I buy handspun in this market and give from 16d. to 18d. for the best kind. It is to be got from 3d. a hank to 4½d. The machinery has thrown our families idle.

The average earnings of all our weavers would not exceed 3s.6d. a week and that is with an attendant as winder. The old weavers were formerly bound as apprentices, generally for three years; at present there is no binding by indenture in this neighbourhood. All girls of 13 to 15 years of age hereabout are weavers and have nothing else to do; their wheels are now thrown by. It would be desirable to make provision for apprenticeship in the weaving trade; it would give better workmen.

Robert Hammond, a weaver from County Londonderry described to the same commission how the weaving trade had declined in his lifetime:
. . . Formerly the small farmers all spun yarn at home and wove besides. They would sow the flax and go through all the processes at home and by the produce of their cloth pay their rents. They lived, that is maintained themselves, in the produce of their farms. In consequence of the decline of this sort of union trade with farming, they cannot now pay their rents and many of the small holdings are now in consequence being consolidated. I have known many such instances in my own place and it is increasing every day.

As a single man, I paid to one of these farmers and weavers £8 a year for my board and lodging; I had my own loom and for the £8 in addition to the board, lodging, and washing, the farmer's family did my winding besides. Very many young single men did the same. At one time I paid but £6 a year for all the above I have named, near Magherafelt. There is but little of this boarding going on at the present moment. It is about four years ago since I boarded for £6. I bought my own materials and sold my own web.

I am a single man still. I could have made a good match since I came to this town but my sweetheart found out that I was a weaver and would not have me. They know the weavers have not the means of keeping a wife and family, and no prudent lass would have one at all.

When I paid £8 a year I could sometimes make 5s. a day. This was about six or seven years ago, or perhaps eight — all by linen weaving, and from hand-spun yarn. I had then two or three good suits of clothes and a watch in my pocket, and sometimes £10 or £12 to the good. Had I ever thought of my trade coming down from 5s. a day to 4s.1d. a week, I should have been more prudent than I was. But I lived respectably and thought myself respectable and that I should never be unable to get a living. I never thought of coming down to my present state.

> When trade it was good, I had money at will.
> Since times is so altered my spirits is dull;
> For I'm a poor weaver and sorely I rue
> The first day that ever my shuttle I threw

The Downfall of Trade (about 1857).

Many people believed that the breakdown of the domestic system would seriously weaken family life. They thought that mills and factories were evil places which would damage both the minds and the bodies of the children they employed. This comment by a clergyman written about 1814 takes a self-righteous and rather patronising view and overstates the case, but many people felt as he did:

. . . . In the former [i.e. the mills] a number of persons of different ages and sexes (some, of consequence, as in all large societies, extremely worthless) are crowded together in one place without guide or guardian over the children, without restraint or obligation on the adult, where each brings his share to the general stock of vice until the accumulation of every wickedness and profligacy, which the varieties of human guilt afford, is complete.

In the latter [i.e. the homes] the industrious parents are cheerfully seated at their employment in the midst of their little family, watching over the conduct and the tempers of their rising offspring, directing them by their counsel, guarding them by their prudence, and teaching them with their own hands the arts of an honest labour.

No one, indeed, can truly appreciate the value of such domestic occupation but he who (like the minister of religion) has daily opportunities of observing that the above is no ideal[ised] picture; and who hourly feels and understands and blesses the effects of an employment which alike preserves the young under a parent's eye, and removes those parents themselves from the contact of vice and corruption.

It is to be hoped that all who thus feel and understand, will heartily join in reprobating every attempt to aggrandise individuals, or even to add to the wealth of the country, by exchanging the happiness and innocence of a diffused, for the wretchedness and profligacy of a collective manufacture.

The poorer classes, however, did not have any choice in the matter.

W. Shaw Mason (ed.), *Statistical survey*, Vol. 1, 343 about parish of Dungiven (3 Vols, Dublin, 1814).

View of the Royal Damask Linen factory at Ardoyne in Belfast, erected in 1819. Although it resembles a workhouse the regime was not so strict: in 1907 it was reported 'any weaver can walk in and out as he likes during working hours (6 a.m. to 6 p.m.)' (Welch collection: Ulster Museum).

They might call the mills and factories 'lock-ups' but where else could they get employment? Agricultural wages were low and jobs on the land were scarce. Therefore the competition for jobs in the factory was so strong that the factory owner could lay down and enforce strict regulations. In fact the nineteenth century, in Britain as well as in Ireland, became increasingly an era of rules and regulations as the middle classes strove to make their working people respectable. Evangelical landlords and employers made themselves responsible for the

Bird's eye view of a workhouse.

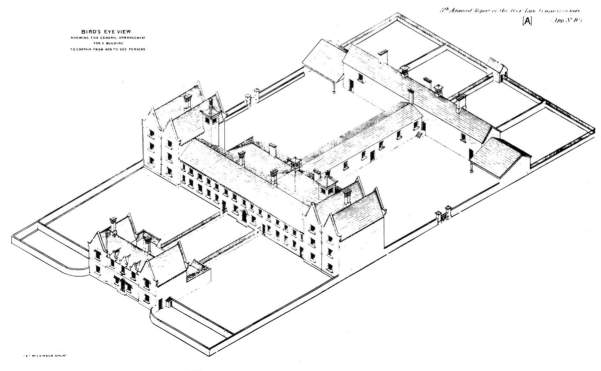

BIRD'S EYE VIEW
SHEWING THE GENERAL ARRANGEMENT
FOR A BUILDING
TO CONTAIN FROM 800 TO 800 PERSONS

5th Annual Report of the Poor Law Commissioners
[A] App N° 10

65

morals of their people. Some landlords in Ulster even appointed moral agents. In the new work-houses, built in the early 1840s, the poor suffered 'minute and regular observance of routine', total separation of the sexes, separation of families, labour, and total confinement. Behind them all stood the government with its new police forces to enforce the law and deal with those who would not, or could not, fit into the new way of life.

The children, however, were never so reluctant as their parents to enter the new power-loom factories. To them it was more natural to go to the factories because they had been born into a world of factories and took them for granted. They knew, too, that earnings there were higher than their parents could make at home. At the new primary schools they had been introduced to the idea of a community regulated by time and a different kind of discipline from that at home. They were subject to a teacher who governed the class and punished their errors

Factory and factory-owner's house near the railway station in Portadown, County Armagh drawn by Robert Donnelly of Portadown. (*Armagh Museum*)

V.

PRACTICAL RULES for the TEACHERS of NATIONAL SCHOOLS.

1. The Teachers of National Schools are required—To keep at least one copy of the GENERAL LESSON suspended conspicuously in the School-room, and to inculcate the principles contained in it on the minds of their Pupils.

2. To exclude from the School, except at the hours set apart for Religious Instruction, all Catechisms and Books inculcating peculiar religious opinions.

3. To avoid fairs, markets, and meetings—but above all, POLITICAL meetings of every kind; to abstain from controversy; and to do nothing either in or out of School which might have a tendency to confine it to any one denomination of Children.

4. To keep the Register, Report Book, and Class Rolls accurately, neatly, and according to the precise form prescribed by the Board; and to enter or mark in the two latter, before *noon* each day, the number of Children in actual attendance.

5. To classify the Children according to the National School Books; to study those Books themselves; and to teach according to the improved method, as pointed out in their several prefaces.

6. To observe themselves, and to impress upon the minds of their Pupils, the great rule of regularity and order—A TIME AND PLACE FOR EVERY THING, AND EVERY THING IN ITS PROPER TIME AND PLACE.

7. To promote, both by precept and example, CLEANLINESS, NEATNESS, and DECENCY. To effect this the Teachers should set an example of cleanliness and neatness in their own person, and in the state and general appearance of their Schools. They should also satisfy themselves, by personal inspection every morning, that the Children have had their hands and faces washed, their hair combed, and clothes cleaned, and, when necessary, mended. The School apartments, too, should be swept and dusted every *evening*, and whitewashed at least once a year.

8. To pay the strictest attention to the morals and general conduct of their Pupils and to omit no opportunity of inculcating the principles of TRUTH and HONESTY : the duties of respect to superiors and obedience to all persons placed in authority over them.

9. To evince a regard for the improvement and general welfare of their Pupils, to treat them with kindness, combined with firmness, and to aim at governing them by their affections and reason, rather than by harshness and severity.

10. To cultivate kindly and affectionate feelings among their Pupils; to discountenance quarrelling, cruelty to animals, and every approach to vice.

11. To record in the Report Book of the School the weekly receipts of School fees, and the amount of all grants made by the Board, as well as the purposes for which they were made, whether in the way of Premiums, Salaries to Teachers, payments to Monitors, or Workmistresses, also School requisites, whether Free Stock or purchased at half-price.

12. To take strict care of the FREE STOCK of Books granted by the Board; and to endeavour to keep the School constantly supplied with National School Books and requisites for sale to the Children, at the reduced prices charged by the Commissioners; also to preserve the invoices for the information of the Inspectors; and whenever requisites (whether Free Stock or purchased) arrive without an invoice, to apply to the manager to whom it is transmitted when the parcel is sent from this office.

13. Should it be intended to close a School for a time not included in the recognised vacations, notice should be given some days previously to the Inspector; and when a Teacher is summoned for training, and means to obey the summons, or intends resigning or removing to another School, he should intimate his intention to the Inspector a month or a fortnight at least before his removal or resignation, in order that the latter may have an opportunity of visiting his School, and reporting upon the state of the Premises, Free Stock, School Accounts, &c.

MAURICE CROSS, } Secretaries
JAMES KELLY, }

Extract from Appendix to the 22nd report of the Commissioners of National Education in Ireland, 1855.

and their misdeeds. School discipline was similar to factory discipline except that workers were fined, often for very trivial offences, instead of beaten. The school bell rang at set times during the day. The children could not come and go as they pleased.

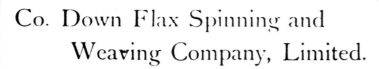

Co. Down Flax Spinning and
Weaving Company, Limited.

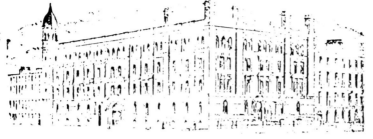

Warehouses and Offices—DONEGALL SQUARE SOUTH, BELFAST.
Telegraphic Address—" LOOP, BELFAST."

AGENCIES—

LONDON	SEVILLE	BERLIN
MANCHESTER	CADIZ	HAMBURG
GLASGOW	VALENCIA	LEIPSIC
NEW YORK	SARAGOSSA	AMSTERDAM
SAN FRANCISCO	LISBON	BRUSSELS
TORONTO	OPORTO	COPENHAGEN
SYDNEY, N.S. Wales	ROME	GOTHENBURG
MELBOURNE	NAPLES	ST. PETERSBURG
BRISBANE	MESSINA	MOSCOW
ADELAIDE	PALERMO	WARSAW
DUNEDIN	MILAN	BUCHAREST
PARIS	TURIN	CONSTANTINOPLE
MADRID	GENOA	ALEXANDRIA
BARCELONA	VIENNA	TUNIS

Advertisement from *The Home and Foreign Linen Trade Directory,* 1892.

68

It was the parents who suffered, particularly if they felt that they were getting too old to change their way of life. They watched helplessly as their standard of living fell from year to year. If their employer, the factory owner, failed to adapt his products to meet the latest demands from the American and Empire markets, or to lower his prices to compete with his rivals, he would not receive enough orders. Yet when he did make these changes he brought more misery to many people. Such was the fate of the handloom weavers who wove linen cambric handkerchiefs. About 1884 a new process enabled the finishing trade about Belfast and Lurgan to produce a cotton handkerchief much cheaper than the linen handkerchief but similar in appearance. In October 1886 Mr Woodgate, an inspector of factories and workshops, wrote this report on the handloom weavers in the counties of Down and Armagh:

Since March 1885 I have visited 785 handloom weavers in their own houses. They all come under the definition of 'Domestic Workshop Act, 1878', being all members of a family working in their own homes. Throughout the Counties Down and Armagh they are very numerous, and I much regret to report this industry, especially the cambric handkerchiefs, is in a very depressed state.

Entry from a register of a north Armagh national school in 1898 mentioning the children of rural weavers. *(PRONI)*

69

I have a letter from one of the largest handkerchief factory owners, in which he informs me that men to whom he gives out yarn to weave in their homes, are only able to earn now on an average 5s 6d a week for eleven hours work a day, and from this has to be deducted the time of the weaver's children in winding for him and getting the yarn ready for weaving; the paste-dressing and spindles used; and the oil used for lamplight, this latter a heavy item in winter months. Nearly all the weavers employ their own children at winding and I have seen them at work at ages ranging from six years and upwards.

The class of goods made by the handloom weaver is chiefly the finest linens and Irish cambric handkerchiefs, table-cloths, etc. I find the number of weavers is gradually falling away through emigration and those at present engaged not bringing up their children to the trade. I have always found the weavers most industrious, hard-working men: never on any of my inspections do I see them idle although they have no master's eye to work under.

I find them one and all most keenly anxious to send their children to school; but with such small earnings it would almost seem an impossibility for all of them to comply with provisions of the Factory and Workshop Act in this respect. The cost of schooling, I find, is a penny a week, and when children have got into the higher grades this is increased to 1½d and 2d a week, and in cases of large families with a father earning 5s 6d a week and having 1s and 1s 6d to pay for rent, it will be seen, after providing food for the body there cannot be much left to provide food for the mind. Nevertheless, I find a large number of the weavers do send their children to school, as they are so anxious they should be educated. The weavers form a very considerable part of the population of the Counties Down and Armagh and it is somewhat surprising that no means have been discussed of enabling them to get free education in extreme cases.

Truck tokens: G.V. Stewart, Lisdourt; Armagh Flax Spinning Mill; Annsborough Stores. *(Ulster Museum)*
Annual report of H.M. inspector of factories and workshops, 31 October 1886.

People in such a miserable situation can be exploited by more ruthless people. All kinds of outworkers suffered in the nineteenth century from the truck system when work was not paid for in cash but in shop goods or in token coins which could be used only in a certain shop. This shop charged higher prices than the village shops. Sometimes such a shop was owned by the factory but others belonged to shop-keepers who acted as agents in rural areas, put out the work, and even compelled the outworkers to take payment in groceries or other goods. In some cases, too, when workers wanted an advance on their earnings before pay-day they were given such 'subs' in tokens known among them (on account of their shape) as 'quoits' or 'washers': at least it prevented them from spending it in the public houses. In 1887 an act was passed which forbade the truck system but it must not have covered the Irish handloom weavers because between 1890 and 1895 several bills were introduced on their behalf into the House of Commons. In 1896 the Truck Act was passed compelling every employer to give each of his workers a copy of the terms under which he was employed and especially setting down what fines he might suffer for negligence or bad workmanship.

The nineteenth century did indeed see the decline of the handloom weavers. Yet, contrary to general belief, the people engaged in the linen industry probably suffered more in the first half of the century than they did in the second. When hand spinning was destroyed by com-petition from machine spinning, very many families suffered their first serious cut in income at a time when the population figures were still rising rapidly. Then the wages for the handloom weavers — men, women, and boys — were forced down by the introduction of the power-loom on a considerable scale in Britain. The Great Famine stirred many people to rouse themselves from the decay of the previous thirty years. Death and emigration reduced the population pressure in the most drastic way possible, and the rise in wages which followed induced many men to set up weaving factories in Ireland. So more work was available for those who were prepared to uproot themselves and move to the new towns. The cities and towns of the east coast grew at the expense of the rest of the country: many of the once prosperous rural areas were left to stagnate.

Selling a roll of hand woven linen in an Ulster town early this century. (Mr Eoin Walsh, Maghera)

Appendix 1

The Linen Weavers Slaying Table,
with Directions and Observations thereon.

PRONI D.562/1321.

Hanks and Cutts in One Pound of whitened Yarn.		Hundreds on the Reed for Yard wide Cloth.		Hanks of Yarn in a Score of Yard wide Cloth.		Hanks and Cuts in One Yard of Yard wide Cloth.		
Hanks.	Cutts.	Hunds.	Hf. Hund.	Hanks.	Cutts.	Hanks.	Cutts.	Quarts.
0	8	6		15		0	9	1
0	9	6	½	16	3	0	9	3
0	11	7		17	6	0	10	2
1	0	7	½	18	9	0	11	1
1	2	8		20		1	0	0
1	4	8	½	21	3	1	3	0
1	6	9		22	6	1	1	2
1	8	9	½	23	9	1	2	1
1	10	10		25		1	3	0
2	0	10	½	26	3	1	3	3
2	3	11		27	6	1	4	2
2	6	11	½	28	9	1	5	1
2	8	12		30		1	6	0
2	11	12	½	31	3	1	6	3
3	2	13		32	6	1	7	2
3	5	13	½	33	9	1	8	1
3	8	14		35		1	9	0
3	11	14	½	36	3	1	9	3
4	2	15		37	6	1	10	2
4	5	15	½	38	9	1	11	1
4	9	16		40		2	0	0
5	1	16	½	41	3	2	0	3
5	5	17		42	6	2	1	2
5	9	17	½	43	9	2	2	1
6	1	18		45		2	3	0
6	9	19		47	6	2	4	2
7	5	20		50		2	6	0
8	2	21		52	6	2	7	2
9	0	22		55		2	9	0
9	10	23		57	6	2	10	2
10	9	24		60		3	0	0
11	9	25		62	6	3	1	2
12	10	26		65		3	3	0
13	11	27		67	6	3	4	2
15	0	28		70		3	6	0
16	2	29		72	6	3	7	2
17	4	30		75		3	9	0

When the Weaver has duly sorted his Yarn, and finds that it is of just Length and Count according to the Statute, he must know how many Hanks and Cutts of that Yarn will make One Pound weight, and with that number he is to enter the First Column of this Table, and when he has found it, or the nearest Number to it, he must carry his Eye on the level to the right, where in the Second Column he will find the Hundreds or Hundreds and Halfs of that Reed in which such Yarn is to be Wrought. In the Third Column he will see how many Hanks and Cutts of such Yarn a Score of Yard-wide Cloth will take. And in the Fourth Column he will find the Hanks, Cutts and Quarters of Cutts, which each Yards length of such Cloth will require. — As for Example. — If he finds that it takes Four Hanks and Five Cutts of his Yarn to make a Pound weight, he will see in the Second Column that it must be wrought in a Fifteen Hundred and a Half Reed. In the Third Column that Thirty Eight Hanks and Nine Cutts thereof will make a Score of Yard-wide Cloth: And by the Fourth Column, that One Hank, Eleven Cutts and a Quarter of a Cutt, will make One Yard of such a set or sort of Linen.

If he thinks fit to add any number of Yards to the above Score, he need not be told that half the above Quantity of Yarn will make Ten Yards more, that the Fourth Part thereof will make Five Yards, and for every other Yard, he is to take so many times the Number he sees in the Fourth Column. — As suppose — He would make a Piece of Linnen Twenty Eight Yards in length, he knows already, that Thirty Eight Hanks and Nine Cutts will make Twenty Yards thereof. That the Fourth Part being Nine Hanks, Eight Cutts, and a Quarter of a Cutt, will make Five Yards, and the Number in the Fourth Column taken thrice (making Five Hanks, Nine Cutts, and Three Quarters of a Cutt) is what the three odd Yards will require. Then by adding these Sums together he will find, that Fifty Four Hanks and Three Cutts of such Yarn will make Twenty Eight Yards of Yard-wide Linnen.

Whence, whoever has a Piece of Linnen Wrought for him has no more to do than to see it measured, and count the Hundreds token'd or mark'd at the end of the Piece, and if they answer according to the Agreement, he may be satisfied the Weaver has done him Justice.

Altho' this Table may be easily understood by any Person who is but indifferently Conversant or Skill'd in the Linnen Trade, yet it may be of service to let the Weavers know upon what Grounds it is Fram'd (which perhaps many of them have not consider'd) and thereby convince them of the absolute necessity of having the Yarn made Statutable, whereby they may suit or fit their Yarn to the Reed very exactly, which can not be done by Guess or Weight.

Every Weaver knows, that his Chain of Warp ought to be longer than the Piece of Linnen he designs to Work, to give allowance for the Shrinking or Running up thereof in the Weaving, Bleaching, etc. Wherefore Four Inches are allow'd or thrown in by this Table for each Yard to be Wrought. So, that the Chain of Warp for a Score of Cloth must be laid on the Warping Barrs Twenty Two Yards and Eight Inches long, and if to this he adds Ten Inches more (as he ought to do) for Looping and fastening his Chain to the Yarn and Cloth Beams, the whole length of his Chain will then be Twenty Two Yards and a Half, whence it may be convenient to make his Barrs so wide as to measure Two Yards and a Half between the Pins on one side, and the Pins on the other, whereby his Chain will take up or fill just Nine Lengths on the Barrs.

He knows likewise, that the Chain of Warp for One Hundred in the Reed consists of Two Hundred Threads in Breadth, and (if for a Score of Cloth) Twenty Two Yards and a Half in Length as abovesaid, and if he Multiplies the one by the other, it will amount to Four Thousand Five Hundred Yards of single Yarn. And if the Yarn of the Weft be of the same Grist and Fineness with the Warp, and struck home, so as to make a true even Square Cloth, it will consist of the like quantity of Yarn, so that both together will amount to Nine Thousand Yards of Yarn exactly.

And when Two Hanks and a Half of Statutable Yarn appear by Computation to contain the like Number of Nine Thousand Yards, he must conclude that Two Hanks and a Half of Yarn will be equal to, and make the Warp and Weft of each Hundred in the Reed for Twenty Yards of Cloth in Length. And that whether the Yarn or Cloth be Finer or Coarser, or Thicker or Thinner, the quantity of Yarn or number of Yards is always the same.

When he reckons also, that a Beer is the Fifth Part of a Hundred in the Reed, and considers that Half a Hank or Six Cutts make the Fifth part of two Hanks and a Half, he must conclude, that they also contain the same Quantity, and are equal to one another in Number of Yards of Yarn, which he ought to take particular notice of, because he can thereby make his Computation and suit or proportion his Yarn to the Reed with all the ease and certainty imaginable; for when he finds by the First and Second Columns, that Yarn (suppose) of Four Hanks and Five Cutts to the Pound must be Wrought in a Fifteen Hundred and Half Reed as already mention'd, then by allowing or reckoning Two Hanks and a Half for each Hundred, or Half a Hank for each Beer, he will find they answer either way and exactly agree with this Table.

By using himself to this manner of Reckoning, the Weaver will very soon overcome all difficulties that can fall in his Way in Adjusting his Yarn to the Reed, let the Piece he intends to work be of what Breadth soever as well as Length, for as soon as he has suited his Yarn to the Reed as already directed, and is resolved what Breadth to make his Cloth, he need only count the Hundreds or Beers on that Part of the Reed fill'd up by the Chain of Warp, and then allow Yarn according as already directed. But to make this Plainer yet, Suppose he is about to Work a Piece of Linnen Thirty Six Yards Long, and Three Quarters and a Half Wide, and would know what Quantity of Yarn it requires, then weighing his Yarn, he finds it must be Wrought in a Thirteen Hundred Reed, but because he intends his Cloth shall be but Three Quarters and a Half wide, he must convert or turn his Hundreds into Beers, which make in all Sixty Five, then taking away the Eighth Part, there remains Fifty Seven Beers, for each of which allowing half a Hank, he will find that Twenty Eight Hanks and a Half will make a Score of Cloth Three Quarters and a Half Wide, then of course Ten Yards will take Fourteen Hanks and Three Cutts, and the Five Yards (being the Fourth Part) will take Seven Hanks, One Cutt and a Half, and the Single Yard about one Hank Four Cutts and a Half, which in all amount to Fifty One Hanks and Three Cutts, and so much Statutable Yarn it will require to make a Piece of Linnen Thirty Six Yards Long, and Three Quarters and a Half Wide.

However Exact and True the above Table and Observations may appear to be, they will be of no Use at all unless the Spinner (whose particular Business it is) Reels up her Yarn into Hanks, Yard and Quarter Long, each consisting of Twelve Cutts, and each Cutt to contain One Hundred and Twenty Threads, as by Law she is oblig'd to do, or forfeit the same. For let the Weaver be ever so Skilful or Perfect in his Trade, yet when he is to Work up Yarn of uncertain and different Lengths and counts, he has no sure Rule to go by, but only to guess at the Quantity and Quality of it, either by his Eye, the grasping of it in his Hand, or judging of it by Weight. Whence our Linnens are frequently spoilt, or abused in the Weaving, so many Complaints made, and disputes arise between the Imployer and the Weaver, not to mention the several ways by which the one (if Dishonest) may Defraud the other, and he not be able either to prevent or discover the Cheat. All which may be easily remedied to the Credit and Improvement of the Linnen Manufacture, would the Spinner and Weaver take care to follow such Rules and Directions as from Time to Time have been prescribed them.
DUBLIN: Printed by Andrew Crooke, Printer to the King's Most Excellent Majesty at the King's-Arms in Copper-Alley, 1723.

Questions

1. How did a weaver know how much yarn he would need to weave a certain kind and length of cloth?
2. How many cutts of yarn were there in a hank?
3. How many pounds of whitened yarn would a weaver need to make a 16^{00} (sixteen hundred) web twenty-five yards long and one yard wide?
4. For what was a clock reel used?
5. What machines did a weaver's assistant use to wind the hanks of yarn on to the pirns (quills or bobbins) for the shuttle?

Appendix 2

Extract from *Belfast News-Letter,* **11 April 1783, reporting capital convictions for robbing bleachgreens.**

BELFAST

At the assizes for the County of Down, which ended on Wednesday last, the following persons were capitally convicted, and received sentence as follows, viz. — Patrick Gordon, otherwise McGurnaghan (to be executed at Drumbridge on Thursday next the 17th. inst.) and Stephen Gordon, otherwise McGurnaghan (to be executed at Castlewellan on Monday next the 14th. inst.) for stealing linen out of the bleachgreen of George and Walter Crawford of Balleivy; George Brown (to be executed at Downpatrick 1st. June next) for stealing linen out of the bleachgreen of Samuel McAlester of Lisnamore; John Wright (to be executed at Banbridge on Monday the 21st. inst.) for stealing linen cloth out of the bleachgreen of James Clibborn at Banbridge, and John Holmes (to be executed at Downpatrick on the 1st. June next) for receiving said linen knowing it to be stolen; and Edward Higgins and Robert Stafford for a burglary in the house of Patrick Crenon of Ballyneran — Stafford to be executed on Saturday se'nnight [week] and Higgins on the 1st. of June next, at Downpatrick. Daniel Murray was found guilty of sheep stealing, and burned in the hand.

It may be hoped that the example of these unhappy wretches will prevent the practice of robbing greens, so injurious to a manufacturer on which the poorest as well as the highest classes of the inhabitants of this country so much depend.

Questions

1. Why were people executed for stealing linen from bleachgreens?
2. Why do you think the authorities executed them in the country towns.
3. Since there was no police force how were the criminals caught?

Appendix 3

A description of the linen industry in County Armagh from an account written in 1795 by Robert Stephenson [MS in Public Record Office of Northern Ireland] PRONI D.562/1270 (see page 36).

. . . . . They carry on some finer branches of the manufacture about Lurgan, the original seat of the manufacture, than in the other parts of the county, such as yard linens, lawns and cambrics, up to high prices. Large quantities of diapers and damasks are manufactured there by weavers, some to sell brown in market, and also by manufacturers who have them bleached and finished fit for exportation before they are sent to market. On the west side of the county about Armagh city and up through the mountains they are entirely employed in making yard wide linens of an excellent quality from about 8d. to 18d. per yard brown, which are in great demand and high estimation; and they have a sufficient number of bleachyards to whiten all their own manufactures on reasonable terms, and large quantities brought into this county by their linendrapers from the neighbouring counties, by means of their great convenience of excellent rivers and a good supply of turf from the mountains or coal from Dungannon colliery.

On taking the most correct account that could then be made of their bleachyards and manufacture in 1771 they were estimated as follows:

On the Callan water and its branches 36 bleachyards whitened yearly 108,500 pieces of yard wides, 25 yards each, estimated on medium at 30s. of value cash £162,750

In other parts of the county 15 bleachyards whitened 54,000 pieces estimated at 40s. each piece. £108,000

Unbleached linens sent yearly to market estimated about. . . . £ 10,000

Total bleached and unbleached sent to market estimated at . . £280,750

It was then estimated that the manufacture of this county had increased nearly two-thirds within the preceding twenty years. The first bleachyard made on the Callan water was in 1743 and there are many new bleachyards added to the above amount since 1771. And by their proficiency in the knowledge of bleaching they can finish, with the same machinery and number of hands, nearly double the quantity of linens. This is effected by using stronger lyes and better ashes and stuffs, by rubbing less and preserving the fabric of the linens better, without aiming at such unnecessary colours on their low priced linens . . . .

Questions

1. Why were so many bleachgreens established in the Callan valley? Why do you think so many had been constructed there by 1771 when the first one had not been erected until 1743?

2. What materials did a bleacher require for bleaching?

3. What great changes were being made in bleaching at this time? Can you find in the book a more exact description of the character of these changes?

Appendix 4

Lines of verse sent with a pack of linen in 1795 from Messrs. Thomas Stott and company, Dromore, County Down, to Mr James Gilmour, Garvagh, County Londonderry.

This morn, Frien' James, we sent a wheen
Of good thick lawns and cambrics thin
To Maister Mirrie's at Belfast
(As we've been wont this sometime past).
The hail[1] are packed in ae stout kist[2]
That nothing hurtful might maelist.

The lawns we fear ye'll no think cheap
Though we by them smal' profit reap.
The cambrics, tho' they luk but lean
Will make a shift[3] to haud their ain.
On baith to this bit paper joined
The bill o' parcels ye will find.
An' we hae placed the fair amount
Right cannily to your account,
Which, if we cast the figures straight,
Is just of pounds four score and eight,
Five Irish siller shillins smug
And six bawbees[4] — to buy a mug.

Now may the pack gang[5] safe to hand,
And like gamecocks their wings expand,
And plaze ye well still as they craw
An' customers an' profit draw
Is the true wish of him wha's faither[6] —
To make ye laugh — put this thegither.

1 whole   4 halfpennies
2 one stout chest   5 go   6 whose father
3 *both* a move *and*
a woman's chemise

1. How were bleached linens packed for transport? Against what harm did they need to be protected?
2. Did you know that the British silver shilling was then worth thirteen pence in Ireland? What was a British guinea worth in Irish money?
3. What do you know about cock-fighting?

Appendix 5

Estimates of annual sales in the Ulster brown linen markets.

1783 figures in PRONI D.562/5596.

1783 & 1803 figures in PRONI D.562/1267.

1816 figures (Corry's report) published in Horner, *The Linen Trade of Europe*, pp.167–9.

1820 figures published in Horner, pp 189–96.

County Antrim	1783	1803	1816	1820
Antrim	2,400	—	—	—
Ahoghill	—	10,800	18,000	13,552
Ballycastle	—	—	—	282
Ballyclare	—	1,200	—	—
Ballymena	52,000	62,400	130,000	55,562
Ballymoney	30,000	12,000	52,800	21,993
Belfast	52,000	156,000	208,000	82,300
Dervock	—	—	—	1,785
Larne	1,200	—	—	—
Lisburn	104,000	145,600	260,000	84,727
Portglenone	7,200	—	28,800	6,892
Randalstown	14,400	24,000	—	6,365
TOTAL	263,200	412,000	697,600	273,458
County Armagh				
Armagh	93,600	208,000	197,600	358,150
Keady	7,800	—	—	—
Lurgan	130,000	130,000	96,200	139,967
Portadown	—	—	7,800	—
Richhill	31,200	5,200	—	—
Tanderagee	26,000	88,400	52,000	56,062
TOTAL	288,600	431,600	353,600	554,179
County Cavan				
Arvagh	—	7,800	20,800	11,953
Ballynagh	—	31,200	26,000	16,256
Ballyhays)				
Ballyconnell)	600	—	—	—
Cavan)				
Cootehill	52,000	114,400	52,000	55,762
Killishandra	15,600	31,200	20,800	15,024
TOTAL	68,200	184,600	119,600	98,995

County Donegal	1783	1803	1816	1820
Ballyshannon	—	—	—	2,005
Letterkenny	6,240	20,800	8,320	6,889
Stranorlar	—	2,600	6,760	4,689
Rathmelton	7,800	26,000	11,830	16,967
Ballybofay, Convoy) and Stranorlar)	2,000	—	—	1,769
TOTAL	16,040	49,400	26,910	32,319

County Down	1783	1803	1816	1820
Banbridge	26,000	52,000	53,976	62,660
Ballynahinch	15,600	7,800	884	1,350
Castlewellan	4,160	7,800	—	—
Downpatrick	15,600	78,000	39,000	4,500
Dromore	—	1,300	—	—
Hillsborough	,18,200	18,200	416	—
Kilkeel	10,400	13,000	20,800	16,500
Kircubbin	—	3,600	7,800	4,500
Newry	52,000	78,000	47,944	70,500
Portaferry	2,400	—	—	—
Rathfriland	5,200	10,400	3,432	15,750
TOTAL	149,560	270,100	174,252	175,760

County Fermanagh	1783	1803	1816	1820
Brookborough	3,600	1,200	—	—
Enniskillen	—	9,600	11,700	20,188
Irvinestown	—	—	—	4,016
Maguire's Bridge Fairs	500	1,200	—	1,560
TOTAL	4,100	12,000	11,700	25,764

County Londonderry	1783	1803	1816	1820
Coleraine	3,900	31,200	44,200	41,184
Dungiven	3,120	5,200	—	1,352
Londonderry	52,000	104,000	58,760	94,630
Kilrea	—	7,200	12,000	14,356
Maghera	6,000	12,000	12,000	—
Magherafelt	7,200	14,400	19,200	19,033
Moneymore	12,000	18,000	30,000	19,171
Newtown Limavady	15,600	26,000	—	2,305
TOTAL	99,820	218,000	176,160	192,031

County Monaghan	1783	1803	1816	1820
Ballibay	26,000	46,800	62,400	46,031
Castleblayney	10,400	26,000	44,200	26,250
Clones	31,200	20,800	33,800	13,372
Glasslough	—	—	12,480	10,140
Monaghan	36,400	57,200	52,000	38,927
TOTAL	104,000	150,800	204,880	134,720

County Tyrone	1783	1803	1816	1820
Aughnacloy	26,000	41,600	—	4,618
Ballygawley	—	—	16,900	6,466
Caledon	3,200	—	—	4,897
Cookstown	6,240	26,000	67,600	43,509
Dungannon	78,000	182,000	208,000	81,295
Fintona	—	12,000	41,600	33,670
Fivemiletown	—	1,800	—	875
Moy	8,400	3,600	—	—
Newtownstewart	31,200	52,000	20,800	32,379
Omagh	—	—	47,840	51,520
Stewartstown	41,600	52,000	32,760	26,831
Strabane	36,400	78,000	123,760	77,502
TOTAL	231,040	449,000	559,260	363,562

Ulster
TOTAL   £1,224,560 £2,177,500 £2,323,962 £1,850,788

Questions
1. List the counties in order of their total figures for each year. Which were the most important and which the least important counties for marketing linens?
2. List the ten most important markets for each year. Which markets were obviously growing or declining during the period?
3. Which of these columns of estimates appears less reliable than the others? Can you suggest any explanations?
4. Can you discover from the tables any signs of the impact of the cotton industry?

Appendix 6

Extract from the 1817 Report of the Linen Board explaining a common malpractice among weavers.

Weavers Selling a Second Time

"A practice prevails among the Linen Weavers of the North of Ireland, of selling their Webs a second time in the same Market, which is very injurious to the regular Buyer, and, of course, injurious to the Trade at large.

"You are aware that when a Linen Market commences, the Buyer stands up on a stool or bench in the Market-place, and the Weaver holds up his Web to him to be examined. If the Buyer approves of it, and both agree about the price, he marks, with a pen or pencil, on the outside fold thereof, his name or signature, and the rate per yard at which the Weaver consents to sell, and he to buy it.

"Every Buyer has some known house or place to which all the Weavers, from whom he purchases Webs in the course of the Market, go to be paid.

"The Weaver who thinks that he has sold too cheap, and that he can get a better price for his Web from some other person, will often contrive to efface or conceal the name or mark of the Buyer to whom he sold it, and will offer it to a new purchaser, and effect a second sale of it with such person. Jobbers, too, will often follow a Weaver whom they suspect to have sold too cheap, and, by offering him some trifling advance, will get possession of the Web, to the loss of the original and regular Buyer . . ."

Questions

1. Why did the draper not just buy the web in the market instead of asking the weaver to meet him later to conclude the bargain?

2. Do you think that this practice of selling a web a second time was dishonest? Why?

3. What penalties would you suggest?

Appendix 7

Extract of several entries for the townland of Derryhale, County Armagh, from an enumerator's notebook compiled for the 1821 census. [MS in Armagh Public Library]

PRONI T.1228 (Derryhale alone of the eight townlands in this typescript was published by T.G.F. Paterson in *Ulster Folklife*, Vol. 7 (1961), 41–50).

13. John Taylor, aged 39, pensioner. Rachel Taylor, wife, aged 40, flax spinner.

14. Patrick McCanna, aged 40, labourer. Ellinor McCanna, daughter, aged 12, flax spinner. John McCanna, son, aged 8. Mary McCanna, sister, aged 47, flax spinner.

15. Charles Wright, aged 51, farmer, 13 acres (Mullentine 6 acres). Elisabeth Wright, wife, aged 51, flax spinner. Thomas Wright, son, aged 23, carpenter (outdoor servant). Mary Wright, daughter, aged 14, flax spinner. Jas. Wright, son, aged 11. Ann Claten, sister-in-law, aged 42, flax spinner (paying for her diet).

16. Alexander Watson, aged 71, farmer, 18 acres. Mary Watson, wife, aged 71, flax spinner. Thos. Watson, son, aged 39, linen weaver. Mary Watson, daughter, aged 32, flax spinner. Alex Wright, aged 5. Wm. Duck, grandson to Al. Watson, aged 18. Wm. Cooney, linen weaver, dieter with Al. Watson.

17. Sanders Watson, aged 30, farmer, 4 acres. Elisabeth Watson, wife, aged 30, flax spinner. Elisagh Watson, daughter, aged 6. Jas. Wat-

son, son, aged 4. Jane Watson, daughter, aged 2. Lucy Watson, daughter, aged 9 weeks.

18. Charles McCleland, aged 40, labourer. Sarah McCleland, wife, aged 41, flax spinner. Elisabeth McCleland, daughter, aged 18, flax spinner.

19. Alex. Jordan, aged 46, flax spinner. Mary Gades, daughter, aged 20, flax spinner. Jas. Clindinney, grandson, aged 3, to Alex Jordan. Wm. George Clindinney, aged 2, grandson to Alex Jordan.

20. John McFadding, aged 21, linen weaver. Elisabeth McFadding, wife, aged 20, flax spinner. Mary McFadding, daughter, aged 1.

21. Uninhabited.

22. Charles Stanley, aged 50, farmer, 35 acres. Alice Stanley, wife, aged 42, flaxspinner. Jas. Stanley, son, aged 22, linen weaver. Elisabeth Stanley, daughter, aged 16, flax spinner. Ann Jane Stanley, daughter, aged 11, at school. Robert Stanley, son, aged 9, at school. Henry Stanley, son, aged 5, at school. Daniel Keenan, aged 16, apprentice to Charles Stanley. Henry Kigan, aged 15, apprentice to Charles Stanley. Thos. Pierson, aged 17, servant boy to Charles Stanley.

23. Jas. Cullen, aged 39, tailor. Sarah Cullen, wife, aged 39, flax spinner. Elisabeth Cullen, daughter, aged 15, flax spinner. Jane Cullen, daughter, aged 13, flax spinner. Mary Cullen, daughter, aged 11. Moriagh Cullen, daughter, aged 8. Ann Cullen, daughter, aged 6.

24. John Metleton, aged 60, farmer (pensioner) 6 acres. Elisabeth Metleton, wife, aged 60, flax spinner. Thos. Metleton, son, aged 28, linen weaver. John Metleton, son, aged 14, linen weaver.

25. John Steenson, aged 21, farmer, 6 acres. Ann Steenson, wife, aged 20, flax spinner.

26. Jas. Dollar, aged 50, linen weaver. Mary Dollar, wife, aged 34, flax spinner. Wm. Dollar, son, aged 14, linen weaver. Martha Dollar, daughter, aged 12, flax spinner. Catherine Dollar, daughter, aged 9. Elisabeth Dollar, daughter, aged 7.

Questions

1. Did any of the women weave?
2. What is the age of the youngest person engaged in flax spinning? in weaving?
3. Why are there more spinners than weavers?
4. Write a description of the Stanley family (No. 22). What suggests that they might be wealthier than the other families?
5. Do you think that most of these people depended on the linen industry for their livelihood?

Appendix 8

Thomas Beggs,
The Auld Wife's Address to her Spinning Wheel

Frae Tibbie Gordon I gat this wheel,
   An' then I was young, an' my face was fair,

The poetical works of Thomas Beggs, Ballyclare (1789–1847), Linenhall Library N 13037.

An' since the first day she cam' into my shiel,[1]
    We aye had something to keep an' to spare.
On the wintry night by the clear ingle side,
    My wee bit lamp hung laigh in the lum;[2]
An' I sung my sang, an' my wheel I plied,
    An' Rorie was pleased wi' the hartsome hum
But now upon her I maun spin nae mair,
An' it mak's my heart baith sorry an' sair.

Now fare thee weel, my cantie wee wheel,
    In age an' youth my staff an' my stay,
How gladly at gloamin, my kind auld chiel
    Has reeled our pirn, sae bonnie an' blae
But men o' cunning, an' pelf,[3] an' pride,
    Hae made thee a useless thing to me;
For they carena what puir bodies betide,
    Or whether they live on the yirth or die.
Now the feck[4] o' my fare is a heart fu' o' wae
An' the fourth o' a groat is the wage o' a day.

The mountain lass, at her wee bit wheel,
    How blythe was her e'e, an' how rosy her cheek!
Her bosom was white, an' her heart was leal,[5] —
    Her mien it was modest, her manner was meek;
But now the pert maidens, wha ply in the mill,
    How wan is their visage,—how dim is their e'e
For the ban they maun bide is enough to chill
    The spring o' the heart an' to deaden their glee:
To toil for men that are hard to please,
In a hot-bed rank wi' vice an' disease.

An' when they speak, it maun be wi a squeal;
    They maun rise an' rin at the toll o' the bell,
An' brook the insult o' a tyrant an' de'il,
    An' the jargon they hear is the language o' hell
To breed a bit lassie in sic a vile place,
    Instead o' her ain father's cot on the green,
It puts the puir thing in a pitifu case—
    Ah! black was the day when they made the
    machine.
It has added mair pelf to the hoards o' the great
And left those that were low in a far lower state.

But weel I remember langsyne, that I,
    When Rorie had little outbye to dae,
Gat aye meat enough an' some claes[6] forbye,
    By keepin' thee busy, an' birrin' away;
An' what though we never could boast o' our gear
    An' what tho' we never were blest wi a bairn;
For cauld or hunger we hadna to fear,
    An' I sung my sang, an' I spun my yarn;

But nae mair for mysel' can I provide,
In these wearifu' days o' poortith[7] an' pride,

An' when I was rade, an' hale, an' young,
   My thread cam' level, an' fine as a hair,
An' the kitten purred, an' the cricket sung,
   An' the care o' my heart, was a lightsome care.
Now men ha'e erected a new ingine,
   An' left but little for us to earn,
An' little for me but to pinch an' to pine';
   I wish I had died when I was a bairn,—
For my guid auld man he has breathed his last,
An' I on the cauldrife[8] warld am cast.

An' now the poke an' the staff I maun tak'
   An' wander awa', an amous to beg,
For a plack[9] in the day is the maist I can mak',
   When I ca' at my wheel till I'm bln' as a cleg,
An' work till the witching hour o' the night,
   A time rather late for a thing like me;
But the guid auld times are gane out o' sight,
   An' it mak's the saut tear aften start to mine e'e;
For lords o' the Mill and Machine ha'e decreed
   That bodies like me maun beg their bread.

Questions

1. What did the old woman blame for the decline in hand-spinning? How accurate was she?

2. What was her opinion of the spinning mills?

3. Where have you seen the argument in verses 3 and 4 expressed in different words elsewhere in the book? Which of the two is more effective?

| [1] cabin, hut | [3] wealth | [5] loyal | [7] poverty | [9] mouthful |
| [2] chimney | [4] portion | [6] clothes | [8] chilly | |

Appendix 9

Edward Sloan

The Weaver's Triumph   From *The Bard's Offering*, (1854).

It was but yestreen I had oot my bit claith, man,
   Tuk it under my arm, doun tae Balford I went,
Untae the Braid Square, tae wee cockit Rab's warehouse—
   For a trifle o' cash, man, it was my intent.
My noodle bein' reeming wi' stoups o' guid liquor,
   I marched in fu' stately and throwed the dud doun,
Whan a cock-o'-the-north o' a foreman, ca'd Hudson,
   Whispered tae his employer — 'We'll gi'e him a croon.'

My wee bit o' labour bein' thrown on the counter,
    Wi' butterfly's een tae examine't he goes;
He hemmed and he ha'd, and he swore it was shameless,
    Syne oot wi' his snoot-cloot and dighted his nose.
He swore that the warp would have been better by double—
    For their penny collars 'twas nae use ava;
Though the price o' my labour was just half-a-guinea,
    He would gi'e me a shilling and let me awa.

I glowered at the ape wi' twa een like red cinders,
    While wee cockit Rab at his knavery did wink;
Quo' I, "Honest foreman, ye ha'e turned a barber,
    Tae shave simple weavers sae neatly, I think;
But haud ye, a jiffey, my potstick-legged callan—
    For my nine-and-sixpence I'll gi'e ye some fun:
I'll ca' doun your betters tae think on your capers,
    And see if you'll rob me, you half-stocked gun."

Noo, twa honest neebours together convened;
    And examined it weel, frae beginning tae end;
And the verdict they gi'en was, "Return him his money,
    Or before Parson Wilkins* you'll ha'e tae attend."
My money I pouched wi' a rollickin' smirk—
    Oh! what was the look that his foremanship gi'en!
Quo' I, "Honest foreman, act somewhat mair justly:
    You see arbitration's but seldom your frien'."

Noo, some o' my neebours mayna ken this same foreman,
    But I'll draw you his portrait as weel as I can,
Though it's nae easy job for a puir, simple weaver,
    As I would wrang him greatly tae ca' him a man:
His face—it's the texture and shape o' a monkey's;
    Each cheek would hold neatly a shilling o' pence;
A' the wit that he has in his weel-theekit noodle's
    What oor neebour Tam ca's a "guid griping sense."

He's like—but why need I attempt tae describe him—
    The pen o' a Buffon would soon be tae blame;
Some day, when auld Nature has been busy working,
    She has tossed by the gruns—made him oot o' the same.
Fareweel tae you, Robin; adieu tae your foreman—
    A pair o' sweet rascals you are, I declare;
It's a pity tae waste pen and ink on sic creatures—
    Guid-bye tae you, neebours, I'll noo say nae mair.
*A magistrate

Questions

1. Can you tell whether this weaver was independent or had taken work from 'wee cockit Rab'?

2. How did the hero save himself from being cheated by the foreman?

3. What do you think really happened at the warehouse?

Appendix 10

Anon.,

On Mr Jacob Orr's Spinning Mill [Armagh Museum]

As I silently lay by a large flowing stream,
A youth and young maiden did rove by the same,
He asked her the cause of such noise o'er the hill,
And she answered, it's music from Mr Orr's Mill.

Behold yon fine object appears in the air,
You'll find great industry is carried on there;
My master has agents his orders to fill,
Mr Henry, young Wright, and the Clerk of the Mill.

And hundreds beside me who would have been poor,
And forced out to wander from door unto door,
Were it not for the Coin which is cast by his Mill,
And marked with the beautiful stamp, Laurelhill.

When he came to our City this building to raise,
He was met by all classes who on him did gaze,
And a great deputation was there to fulfil
Their congratulations for this Spinning Mill.

Said he pretty maiden since you have came here
With smiles so enchanting and looks so sincere,
We can rest here a while till the water grows still,
To we hear the fine music that comes from Orr's Mill.

I wish I was working with you for one year
In this splendid building which you hold so dear,
I could dress the lint, while the bobbins you'd fill,
I would love to be working in this Spinning Mill.

The Manager there you will find he's not shy,
I'll do my endeavour to get you employ,
Dunlop and young Henry has charge of the till,
By which you can live, as it's marked Laurelhill.

She got him employment, he works at his trade,
In less than 12 months his young bride she was made,
And now the first baby sings out with fine skill,
Mamma, when will Da bring me sweets from Orr's Mill.

So all you young men who may seek for a wife,
I hope you'll take notice to Mill Factory life,
When the engine does send forth a whistle most shrill,
You'll have such spare moments round this Spinning Mill.

Or you can have a walk by the Old Callan side,
And view with delight this young man and his bride,
You may there see them seated on Stanley's green hill,
Where she showed him the Chimney of Orr's Spinning Mill.

Health to Mr Orr as each fortnight goes round,
Is toasted with joy where his workmen abound,
Praise to him is due for exerting his skill,
And relieving the poor by his great Spinning Mill.

And now in conclusion a health may go round
To this benefactor of country and town,
And his loving Consort ere I drop my quill
May they flourish with honour while in Laurelhill.

Questions
1. What benefits had the mill brought to the neighbourhood?
2. Why does the author write: 'Health to Mr Orr as each fortnight goes round' and not 'each week'?
3. To what do the following lines refer: 'Were it not for the coin which is cast by his mill, And marked with the beautiful stamp, Laurelhill.'? Does this suggest any date for the poem?
4. What was the official name for this mill?

Appendix 11

Regulations and conditions of the contract of service between W. Liddell and Co. Ltd. and all persons working in the Donacloney power-loom factory [MS in Public Record Office of Northern Ireland] PRONI D.1882/2/1.

Note

In the following rules the word 'worker' includes all persons employed in the Donacloney part of the factory and the said W. Liddell and Co. are described as 'the employers'.

1. *Hours:* All workers shall start to work each morning at six o'clock and continue in employment till 5 30 pm except on Saturdays when the factory closes at 12 30 pm. Three-quarters of an hour is allowed for breakfast and the same time for dinner except on Saturdays when only half an hour is allowed for breakfast.

2. *Wages:* The wages will be paid on Thursday in each week and on each Monday the workers shall give in all passbooks or cards in their possession to the clerk. Payment will be made according to the scale entered in the passbooks or cards: and when it is intended to alter the rate of wages the new scale shall be entered in the passbooks or cards at least 14 days previous to its coming into operation. The passbooks or cards shall remain in the employers' custody but during working hours shall be accessible to the workers.

3. *Deposit:* One week's wages or in the case of piece workers the value of one week's work shall be retained by the employers and (unless forfeited) will be paid to the workers at the end of the contract of service.

4. *Notice:* All workers desirous of leaving the factory shall, on a pay day, give to the manager 14 days notice of their intention to leave and the like notice will be given by the employers before discharging any worker.

5. *Stoppage for repairs:* Should the works be stopped for repairs or any accidental cause during the continuous period of 3 days, workers shall have the option of taking other employment upon intimation of their intention so to do, being left with the clerk or manager; and piece workers having to wait for work for 3 consecutive days shall have the like option on giving intimation as before provided. Note. Rules 4 and 5 shall not apply to workers employed for a longer period than 14 days.

6. *Short time:* To meet exigencies of trade the employers shall have it in their power, upon a notice of 3 days, to put the workers or any number of them in short time, but such limitation of time or the want of continuous employment from the causes specified in Rule 5, shall not entitle the workers to make any claim against the employers for compensation or otherwise.

7. *Fines:* It is a special condition of the contract between the employers and workers that upon a worker committing any of the acts or defaults hereafter specified, the employers or others authorised and acting in their behalf, shall for each and every such act or default retain out of the wages of such worker the sum of money or other compensatory deduction herein underset opposite to such act or default; and further (excepting in the cases embraced in second class) not only shall they be entitled to make deduction from the wages as above provided, but the employers or the manager may also dispense with the notice provided by Rule 4 and instantly dismiss the worker committing such act or default from their employment; and in every case an entry of the amount to be retained from or paid by a worker, or of the dismissal of a worker shall be made in the memorandum book or books kept in the cloth receiving room, or office, as the case may be, and also in the worker's passbook.

Fines: Class 1: Being absent from work without leave for more than 2 hours; being absent through sickness without sending immediate notice to the manager; introducing a stranger into the works without leave from the employers or manager; using improper language to anyone; interrupting the workers at the work, or refusing to obey the orders of the employers or overseer; smoking tobacco, bringing matches or liquor into or being the worse of liquor within the works.

For each such act or default the wages retained as provided by Rule 3.

Trespassing into any part of the factory other than that in which the worker is employed; the shifting by weavers of their weights, or altering any part of their looms without leave; making use of the yarn waste; disfiguring the walls or any part of the work by writing or otherwise.

For each such act one shilling.

Wilfully or negligently injuring or breaking the machinery or wasting injuring or destroying cloth, yarns or other materials.

The value of the machinery, material or cloth injured or destroyed.

Fines: Class 2: Being absent from work at the time of starting, either in the morning or after meals — For every five minutes one penny.

Leaving work during working hours without a pass from the overseer — One Shilling.

Entering to or returning from the work by any other access save the north door, or if entering or returning in a noisy and disorderly manner; knitting, sewing or reading while at work in the factory; neglecting to keep the machinery under the worker's charge clean and properly oiled; allowing pirns, bobbins, yarn or waste to lie about the floor; neglecting to sweep passages and floor under looms and frames at 7 o'clock a.m. 12 o'clock noon and 5 o'clock p.m.; widening gas burners or neglecting to shut off the gas — For each such act sixpence.

The marking a wrong number of pieces, or keeling a wrong length, by a warper or dresser — one shilling or in the option of the employers, the loss caused by such carelessness.

Neglecting to give notice to the manager or overseer immediately on the discovery by the worker that the materials or preparation is faulty — The loss caused by the neglect.

The making by a weaver of insufficient cloth, by its being thin, mixed, floated or with shires, under picks or gear gauls, or by the temples working over the breast beam, allowing the rods to work too near the heddles or harness or any other avoidable cause; or measuring wrong lengths — The amount of damage done.

Failure on the part of an overseer or tenter to report to the masters or manager any of the acts or defaults above specified so soon as known to him — Whatever loss may be caused by such neglect.

8. *Delivery of work:* No manufactured article, or other work, shall be considered as delivered over by the workers to the employers until such article or other work shall in its order have been examined and passed by the manager or cloth inspector.

9. The enforcement of any of the foregoing rules shall not relieve any worker of his or her legal obligation to continue and complete the stipulated term of service.

N.B. All persons employed in the factory whether under written agreement or otherwise, shall be held to have acquiesced in and to have been engaged by and according to the foregoing rules as conditions of their contract of service; any worker who may feel aggrieved by them having it in his or her power to leave the work by giving the prescribed warning.

W Liddell and Co Ltd
Donacloney 1890 [County Down]

Questions

1. How many hours were worked each week by an employee in Donacloney factory?

2. If you had been the factory manager at Donacloney how would you have justified imposing fines on the workers? Do you think the fines were unjust?

Appendix 12

From poems (1900).

Thomas Given,
The Weaver Question

We read o' meetings to support
  The risin' nerra-gauge,[1]
Which is to be the strength and fort
  O' every comin' age.

We read o' controversies lang,
    O' puirhoose jaw and vapour,
But seldom does the weavers' wrang
    Bedeck the public paper
        On any day.

Oor wabs are lang an' ill to weave—
    Sometimes the yarn is bad—
Till scanty claes, wi' ragget sleeve,
    Is seen on lass an' lad.
But noo[2] guid fortune we'll attain,
    For orators sae thrifty
Will gar[3] the dreeper clip his chain
    Wa' doon tae twa-an'-fifty
        On ilka day.

Queels[4] maun be wun[5] when claith is wrought,
    An' pickers, shears an' treadles,
Tallow an' temples maun be boucht,
    An' floor tae dress the heddles.
Then meat tae gar the wee yins leeve,
    Maun come as weel's the tackle,
But shure the wages we receive
    Wud hardly buy them treacle
        Tae meal this day.

How aisy 'tis for men tae preach
    Whun riches they hae got,
An' wae self-interest's purse-hurt screech,
    Ca' us a sinful lot.
But, haud a wee! ye men o' wealth!
    Though noo for breath yer pantin',
We ax nae favours gained by stealth—
    It's justice that we're wantin'—
        Nae mair this day.

I ne'er blessed wae gift o' gab,
    Like some great learned men,
Instead o' school, I wove my wab,
    Before that I was ten.
Though noo I'm auld an' gray's my hair,
    I've studied weel the sense o't,
For work let us get wages fair,
    Nae matter 'boot the length o't
        On any day.

[1]narrow-gauge [railway]   [2]now   [3]make   [4]quills   [5]wound

Questions

1. What expenses did a handloom weaver have to take into acount when calculating his actual wages?
2. Explain in your own words what 'weaver question' the poet was discussing.

Handloom Weavers
in the Ulster Linen Industry

A Bibliographical Essay

The pioneer work was Conrad Gill's *The rise of the Irish linen industry* (Oxford, 1925 reprinted 1964), which was based mainly on printed sources. As a lecturer in economic history at Queen's University, Belfast, Gill was interested in the linen industry as Ireland's contribution 'towards that great transformation of industry and society' popularly known as the Industrial Revolution. He wanted not only 'to trace the change from domestic to factory production' but also to discover the role of government and so he paid considerable attention to the history of the Board of Trustees of the Linen and Hempen Manufactures (known as the Linen Board) set up by the Irish Parliament to regulate the industry. This agenda, which was typical of its period, enabled Gill to marshal a great mass of evidence but it over-emphasised some aspects while failing to place the industry insufficiently in its economic and social context. Subsequent research has redressed the balance to some extent.

Gill himself was interested in the origins of the industry but although he made several suggestions he concurred with none, preferring to speculate instead about the significance of systems of land tenure. It was E.R.R. Green in an essay on 'The linen industry in county Down' in his book *The industrial archaeology of county Down*, (Belfast, 1963) who suggested that the industrial development of the region originated with the English and Scottish settlers and their desire to exploit the properties they had acquired. This theory was endorsed by Crawford in a paper on 'The origins of the linen industry in north Armagh and the Lagan Valley' (*Ulster Folklife* 17 (1971)) based on church registers, estate records and memorials of deeds, leases, mortgages, wills and marriage settlements lodged in the Registry of Deeds after it was established in Dublin in 1708. The paper went on to examine an older claim that the industry had been introduced by a colony of Huguenots led by Louis Crommelin and established in Lisburn in 1698. Some time after the publication of this paper David Dickson turned up a letter written from Lisburn in 1697 to the Board of Trade and Plantations reporting that there were then from five hundred to a thousand looms working commercially in the counties of Down, Antrim, Armagh, Tyrone and Londonderry and that County Down produced well-made linens 'little inferior to French cloth.' Such source materials were so profitable that Crawford continued to mine them in another paper on 'Drapers and bleachers in the early Ulster linen industry' discussing commercial and technical progress in the early eighteenth century.

About the same time H.D. Gribbon was engaged in a study of the history of the Linen Board and in 1977 he published a conference paper on 'The Irish Linen Board, 1711–1828' based on its records, pamphlets and the correspondence of John Foster, its most energetic member: unfortunately the manuscript records of the Board before 1784 had been destroyed in the Four Courts fire in June 1922. Although Gribbon came to the conclusion that the Board failed in most of its objectives, he attributed this to inadequacy at administrative level. Nevertheless, throughout the eighteenth century, the Board presided over a successful, expanding industry with the enthusiastic support of the Ulster gentry whose rentals had benefited so much. This support evaporated after the Board in 1782 tried to enforce unpopular laws on the bleachers and thereafter the nucleus of the trade moved from Dublin to Belfast. A growing sense of independence among the bleachers as they developed direct contacts with British customers, left the Board isolated and irrelevant so that the government withdrew its financial support in 1828.

One of the Linen Board policies that had failed in the mid-eighteenth century was its attempt to diffuse the industry throughout the rest of Ireland. The energy with which this policy was pursued is detailed in a series of reports by a certain Robert Stephenson. In his evidence to an Irish House of Commons committee in 1758 Stephenson claimed that in 1741 he 'went apprentice to a linen factor in London, with whom he stayed for four years, then returned into this kingdom, and hath since his return carried on several branches of the linen manufacture, imported great parcels of foreign flax and exported great quantities and various kinds of linen to different parts of the world'. From the early 1750s until the 1790s Stephenson published a considerable number of reports and pamphlets and his work was held in high regard by contemporaries: a study of his writings would throw much fresh light on the textile aspects of the economy of provincial Ireland. Until this appears it is likely that too much reliance will continue to be placed on the comments of Arthur Young when he toured in Ireland in 1776–7. It would be interesting to speculate how much Young's opinions may have been influenced by contemporary pamphlet literature (see for example *Serious considerations on the present alarming state of agriculture and the linen trade, by a farmer* (Dublin 1773) reprinted in *Ulster Folklife* 22 (1987)).

Although the character of the trade varied widely across the northern half of Ireland, success depended in the last resort on the energy and business ability of the bleaching community. A good account of the creation of such a bleaching concern is Amy Monahan's 'An eighteenth century family linen business'. Of especial value is a collection of correspondence (held in PRONI as D.1044) belonging to a major bleacher, Thomas Greer of Dungannon (1724–1803), and his career has been written up for a PhD thesis presented to The Queen's University of Belfast by John W. McConaghy in 1979. One of his market account books has been analysed by W.H. Crawford in 'The market book of Thomas Greer, a Dungannon linendraper, 1758–9.' The most comprehensive survey of the evolution of the provincial linen markets is contained in Crawford's article 'The evolution of the linen trade of Ulster before industrialisation.'

The technical side of the industry has been well researched over the past thirty years. Rodney Green's pioneer study, *The industrial archaeology of county Down*, was followed in 1969 by H.D. Gribbon, *The history of water power in Ulster*. Then in 1980 came the publication of W.A.

McCutcheon, *The industrial archaeology of Northern Ireland*. While both Green and Gribbon in the relevant chapters of their books concentrated on the mills and factories powered by water, McCutcheon dealt also with the hand skills and tools needed for the dressing of the flax as well as spinning and weaving. In 1984, Aileen L'Amie added further to our understanding by her M.S.Sc. thesis on 'Chemicals in the eighteenth century Irish linen industry': she makes a strong case in arguing that the use of a range of chemicals for bleaching was more significant in increasing the output of the bleachgreens than even the use of water power. All aspects of the industry were accurately depicted in a series of twelve engravings made by William Hincks and published in London in 1783: a detailed commentary on these prints was edited by R.A. Gailey and it provides valuable comments about everyday life throughout the province.

Even a glance at the Hincks prints makes us aware of the folk who worked in the industry. Although little information survives about them as individuals, there is a considerable amount of evidence about their social history and the problems of everyday life. Some of the best information is to be found in the series of statistical surveys prepared for most of the counties of Ireland under the aegis of the Dublin Society (later the Royal Dublin Society) and commencing publication in 1801. Their great virtue lies in placing the linen industry in perspective so that its complex relationship with agriculture can be understood better: anyone who studies them will not make the mistake of finding a proletariat emerging the weavers of north Armagh while overlooking the cottier status of weavers in south Antrim. Sir Charles Coote's *Statistical survey of the county of Monaghan* has an especially good 'sketch of the linen manufacture, from the importation of the flax seed, until the sale of the linen in a home or foreign market'. Because Coote wrote reports also for counties Cavan and Armagh it is possible to discover important differences in social structure between the three counties. Whereas in north Armagh especially, the weavers in general held their small farms directly from substantial landowners, elsewhere the more substantial weavers tended to parcel out their farms among cottier weavers and to insist on payment by weaving. In his memoir on Tyrone John McEvoy provides us the best discussion of the impact of handloom weaving on a variety of rural communities: those where farms were 'compactly divided' and fenced; those were farmers exploited 'under-tenants'; and those were farms had already become too small to be profitable.

The picture of the subsequent development of the handloom weaving industry and the linen trade before the invention of the wet-spinning process in 1825, was clouded by Gill's attempt to trace the rise of a putting-out industry at the expense of the public markets. In 1988, however, in a paper 'That evolution of the linen trade of Ulster before industrialisation' Crawford used two government reports, dated 1822 and 1825 respectively, to show that the public markets still retained the allegiance of the great majority of weavers, as well as the bleachers who sent their agents throughout the province. Of course, government reports of this kind concentrate on the broad picture at the expense of the fringes of the trade where groups such as the keelmen operated (see page 19).

93

There is no doubt that the character of handloom linen-weaving was altered completely by the introduction of the wet-spinning process. They were forced by economic pressures to accept the employment conditions that had evolved in the cotton industry in Belfast over the previous forty years. The rapid disappearance of independent handloom weavers is spelt out in great detail in the government reports on the handloom weavers in 1840. They can be supplemented from Ordnance Survey Memoirs of the '30s, some of which are excellent. Yet it is easy to overlook the importance of the handloom-weaving industry that survived. The output of the new wet-spinning mills would not have saved the industry from its more advanced English and Scottish competitors if there had not been such a large number of weavers of fine linens in Ulster. We still have to explain their origins. Our only figure is 13,000 cambric weavers is 1854 according to the Lisburn historian of the industry, Hugh McCall.

It was reckoned that about two-thirds of these weavers were engaged in weaving handkerchiefs while the remainder wove about 4.5 million yards of cambric per annum for printed ladies dresses. The introduction of powerlooms in the 1850s forced down their standard of living and so throughout mid-Ulster communities of handloom-weavers were decimated as the younger people moved away to the towns. Crawford's paper on 'A Handloom weaving community in County Down' studies the impact of change on three townlands in north-west Down where the problem of unemployment was eased a little by the establishment of a Swiss embroidery school under the aegis of the Department of Agricultural and Technical instruction. The only major documentary source for the study of these weavers is the series of annual reports by the factory inspectors published in the parliamentary papers. These have been well used in the preparation of Marilyn Cohen, 'Working condition and experiences of work in the linen industry: Tullylish, county Down' which refers to employment in factories, mills and bleachgreens as well as the homes.

CLARKSON, L.A., AND COLLINS, B., 'Proto-industrialization: Lisburn 1820–21' in P. Deyon and F. Mendels, *La Protoindustrialisation: théorie et réalité* (Budapest, 8th International Congress of Economic History, 1982).

CLARKSON, L.A., 'The environment and dynamic of pre-factory industry in Northern Ireland' in P. Hudson, ed., *Regions and industries: a perspective on the industrial revolution in Britain* (Cambridge, 1989).

COHEN, M., Working conditions and experiences of work in the linen industry: Tullylish, county Down', *Ulster Folklife*, 30 (1984) pp.1–21.

COLLINS, B., 'Proto-industrialisation and pre-Famine emigration', *Social History*, 7, 1 (1982)), pp.127–46.

COOTE, C., *A statistical survey of the county of Monaghan* (Dublin, 1801).

COOTE, C., *A statistical survey of the county of Cavan* (Dublin, 1802).

COOTE, C., *A statistical survey of county of Armagh* (Dublin, 1804).

CRAWFORD, W.H., 'The market book of Thomas Greer, a Dungannon linen draper, 1758–9', *Ulster Folklife*, 13 (1967), pp.54–60.

CRAWFORD, W.H., 'The origins of the linen industry in north Armagh and the Lagan valley', *Ulster Folklife*, 17 (1971), pp.42–51.

CRAWFORD, W.H., 'Drapers and bleachers in the early Ulster linen industry' in L.M. Cullen and P. Butel, eds, *Négoce et industrie en France et en Irlande aux xviie et xixe siècles* (Paris, 1980), pp.113–9.

CRAWFORD, W.H., 'The evolution of the linen trade of Ulster before industrialisation', *Irish economic and social history*, XV (1988), pp.32–53.

CRAWFORD, W.H., 'The political economy of linen: Ulster in the eighteenth century', in C. Brady, M. O'Dowd, and B. Walker, eds, *Ulster: an illustrated history* (London, 1989), pp.134–57.

CRAWFORD, W.H., 'Women in the domestic linen industry' in M. MacCurtain in M. O'Dowd, eds, *Women in early modern Ireland* (Edinburgh, 1991), pp.255–64.

CRAWFORD, W.H., 'A handloom weaving community in county Down', *Ulster Folklife*, 39 (1993).

DUBOURDIEU, J., *A statistical survey of the county of Down* (Dublin, 1802)

DUBOURDIEU, J., *A statistical survey of the county of Antrim* (Dublin, 1812)

GAILEY, R.A., 'The Ballyhagan [county Armagh] inventories, 1716–40', *Folklife*, 15 (1977), pp.36–64.

GAILEY, R.A., ed., 'Illustrations of the Irish linen industry in 1783, by William Hincks', *Ulster Folklife*, 23 (1977), pp.1–32.

GILL, C. *The rise of the Irish linen industry* (Oxford, 1925, reprinted 1964).

GREEN, E.R.R., 'The cotton hand-loom weavers in the north-east of Ireland', *Ulster Journal of Archaeology*, 3rd series, 7 (1944), pp.30–41.

GREEN, E.R.R., *The Lagan valley 1800–1850: a local history of the industrial revolution* (Manchester, 1949).

GREEN, E.R.R., *The industrial archaeology of county Down* (Belfast, 1968).

GREER, J., R*eport of the state of the linen markets in the province of Ulster* (Dublin, 1784: a copy annotated with figures and comments relating to 1803 is in PRONI D.562/6225.

GRIBBON, H.D., *A history of water power in Ulster* (Newton Abbot, 1969).

GRIBBON, H.D., 'The Irish linen board, 1711–1828' in L.M. Cullen and T.C. Smout, eds, *Comparative aspects of Scottish and Irish economic and social history* (Edinburgh, 1977), pp.77–87.

HORNER, J., *The linen trade of Europe during the spinning wheel period*, (Belfast, 1920).

HUTTON, A.W., ed., *Arthur Young's tour in Ireland* (2 vols., London, 1892).

JOHNSTON, J. 'Flax and linen in the Clogher valley', *Clogher Record* XI, no. 2 (1983), pp.287–94.

L'AMIE, A., 'Chemicals in the eighteenth-century Irish linen industry' (M.S.Sc. thesis, Queen's University, Belfast, 1984).

MCCALL, H., *Ireland and her staple manufactures* (3rd ed., Belfast, 1870).

MCCONAGHY, J.W., 'Thomas Greer of Dungannon (1724–1803) — Quaker linen merchant' (Ph.D. thesis, Queen's University, Belfast, 1979).

MCEVOY, J.A., *A statistical survey of the county of Tyrone* (Dublin, 1802: reprinted 1991).

MCPARLAN, J., *A statistical survey of the county of Donegal* (Dublin, 1802).

MONAHAN, A., 'An eighteenth-century family linen business', *Ulster Folklife* 9 (1963), pp.30–45.

MULLIN, T.H., *Aghadowey [county Londonderry]* (Belfast, 1972).

MURNANE, P. & J.H., 'The linen industry in the parish of Aughnamullen, county Cavan and its impact on the town of Ballybay 1740 to 1835', *Clogher Record*, XII, No. 3 (1987), pp.334–68.

O'MORDHA, P., 'The linen industry in the Clones area (1660–1840), *Clogher Record*, X, no.1 (1979), pp.144–53.

SMYTH, W.J., 'Flax cultivation in Ireland: the development and demise of a regional staple' in W.J. Smyth and K. Whelan, eds, *Common ground: essays on the historical geography of Ireland presented to T. Jones Hughes* (Cork, 1988).

SOLAR, P.M., 'A Belgian view of the Ulster linen industry in the 1840s', *Ulster Folklife*, 34 (1988), pp.16–25.

SOLAR, P.M. 'The Irish linen trade, 1820–1852', *Textile History*, 21, 1 (1990), pp.57–85.